Home Cooking with Mushrooms

Outstanding Recipes from Morgan Hill's Mushroom Mardi Gras, Mushroom Farmers, Families, and Chefs

twin falls press

P.O. Box 2001
Morgan Hill
California 95038

First Printing, May 1993

Cover and Interior Design by Steve Virgilio, V.I.P. Graphics

Front Cover and Interior Illustrations by Jim Foder

ISBN: 0-9636578-8-7

Library of Congress Catalog Card Number: 93-60494

Printed in the United States of America

Dedication

To those who cook for themselves and others,
filling kitchens with the familiar clatter of
pans and comforting aroma of home cooking.
For our mothers and grandmothers who cooked for us.

Acknowledgments

We salute the Mardi Gras Cook-off and Favorite Recipe Contest winners featured in this book. We are grateful for the recipes of the home cooks and professional chefs, as well. A special thanks to Art Lopez of Monterey Mushrooms and George Boro of B&D Mushrooms, both of Morgan Hill, California, for their tours and expertise in mushroom farming. Thanks also to Morgan Hill's Mushroom Mardi Gras Board and Lorraine Welk who encouraged us to write this book. We appreciate our daughter, Noelle Nicholson, for her energy and enthusiasm which sees us through the Mardi Gras weekend every year. Arlene Adamson, our transcriptionist, deserves a great deal of credit for helping us meet publishing deadlines. For copy editing and food preparation advice, we thank Roland Stewart, Beth McGhee, Audry Yanes, and Merilyn Meredith. Special thanks also to our friends Merrill Sanders, Donna and Bill Dowdney, Mark and Lupe Levine, Andrée Abecassis, Emmett Scott, and Monserrat Fontes for their helpful advice and support.

Preface

H OME COOKING WITH MUSHROOMS is a collection of recipes from Morgan Hill's Mushroom Mardi Gras Cook-off and Favorite Recipe contests, and collected recipes from the mushroom growers' industry. We added, as well, a generous helping of wonderful recipes from chefs and household cooks whose practical, charming, and sometimes ingenious creations enrich the book's repertoire of mushroom cookery. Caught up in the excitement, we spent many happy and delicious hours in our country kitchen testing recipes and creating our own. The possibilities are endless!

Newcomers to the city of Morgan Hill, we went to our first Mushroom Mardi Gras to get acquainted with local culture. What we remember most is the mouth-watering fragrance of fresh, cultivated mushrooms being sautéed, baked, marinated, and deep fried. Rows of kiosks set up in Nelson Park sold inexpensive mushroom delicacies to long lines of enthusiasts. Between concerts, crafts, and visits to the wine tent, we kept going back for different mushroom specialties.

Home style chefs that we are, it was only natural to look for the cookbook that would help us recreate the delights we had sampled. To our amazement, we found no such book. Later, we decided to write a cookbook that would celebrate the Mardi Gras, mushroom farming, and home cooking.

Our main goal is to have fun. In keeping with the spirit of the Mardi Gras, the book focuses on cultivated mushrooms in old and new recipes. To please a wide audience, the choices range from ambitious gastronomic creations to simple, elegant fare. We even added a section called "Convenient Recipes" for the times when cooks prefer short-cuts or last-minute ideas.

Cooking with mushrooms can be a challenge to those who want to make them more of a central ingredient. This book builds the mushroom user's confidence and expertise by including sections on buying, storing, preparing, and preserving them. We hope the special cooking tips and essay on wine and mushrooms heighten your experience. The text and art in the book reflect our joy in researching and writing it, and finding that mushrooms are many things to many people: whimsy, science, art, folklore, and best of all, food.

Contents

Kitchen Reverie

The ground lies damp,
The air blows chill.

I stay indoors that
I may heal.

Sometimes I must
Remain quite still.

Yet, I rejoice to
Cook one meal.

Sandra L. Stewart

White Mushroom
Agaricus bisporus

Shiitake Mushroom
Lentinus edodes

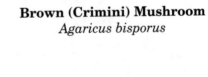

Brown (Crimini) Mushroom
Agaricus bisporus

Oyster Mushroom
Pleurotus ostreatus

Home Cooking with Cultivated Mushrooms

Many of the suggestions in this book refer to the common white (*Agaricus bisporus*) mushroom. However, throughout the discussion there will be information about the three other cultivated mushrooms that are also the subject of this book, the brown (Crimini) mushroom, sometimes called the Italian Brown, the Oyster variety, and the Shiitake.

What is home cooking with mushrooms? What we know about nutrition and food has come full circle, back to home cooking. Yes, we're talking about those old-time standards you used to eat at Grandma's house: homemade bread and noodles, potatoes, beans, rice, and the unforgettable apple pie. Those were the days before our fast-track society began eating more liquid meals and processed foods. In the last twenty years or so, eating out has become convenient, and it seems the whole idea is to get away from home-cooked foods. In some of the most fashionable restaurants, foods have been puréed, salted, sweetened, fattened, and colored as to be almost unrecognizable as whole, familiar foods.

Happily, that trend is changing. Many nutritionists, chefs, and consumers agree that as a style, home cooking with its emphasis on whole foods is more flavorful, more nutritious, and much more economical. Unfortunately, much of the home cooking many of us remember was neither tasty nor nutritious. How can we forget the cauliflower boiled to a bland mush? Or the overcooked pork chops swimming in grease? The art of contemporary home cooking calls for methods of preparation that enhance the flavor, texture, and nutrition of whole foods. Today, so-called "peasant" foods have become the gourmet meals of many health-conscious people. We are beginning to understand world-wide that the diets of our predecessors and that of many poor, agricultural communities around the world have sustained lives longer and been more successful at preventing cancer and heart disease.

What about the other rewards of home cooking? Love and comfort are the main staples of every home cooked meal. My grandparents were ministers of a church in my small, California hometown. Sunday dinner was nearly as sacred as the morning service. My half American-Indian grandma got up early in the morning on Sunday to prepare food for the afternoon meal. I sat sleepily at the kitchen table in my nightgown while she made stuffing for the roast chickens, rolled out and sliced the noodles, grated cabbage for the cole slaw, pared green apples for the apple crisp, and mixed cornmeal so that later she could make "fried mush," one of her specialties.

While she popped the finished dishes into the oven or refrigerator, my sisters and I dressed in our best clothes and went to Sunday school. Some time near the end of the main service, delectable smells drifted from the parsonage into the windows and doors of the church. Our prayers floated on the aromatic waves of meat roasting gently in an old-fashioned Dutch oven, and the warm, yeasty fragrance of bread rising.

Whether you like to cook or not, I suggest a new approach to an old and honored art. I love to eat gourmet food in wonderful restaurants, too. I challenge you to think of home cooking in a new way—with mushrooms! What a simple way to bring elements of gourmet cooking into your home.

When Timothy, my husband, and I decided to write this book, I had no idea that mushrooms would revolutionize the meals we had prepared for years. With thick, juicy mushrooms added to the vegetables and broth, the pot roast took leave of its stodgy sameness. A banquet of mushroom-centered new dishes sprang from our cutting block, pots, and pans. Books about mushrooms packed our cookbook shelves. Mostly, we improvised, with delightful and tasty results.

The ethnic foods we cook now have a more distinctive, authentic appearance and taste. After all, most of the world has eaten mushrooms for centuries. Our Asian dishes flaunt the Shiitake, and we wouldn't dream of an Italian sauce without mushrooms. Why resist mushrooms any longer? Remember that foods such as tomatoes and garlic took a long time to catch on in the "new world," but when they did, American diets and palates were transformed. Let it be so for the mushroom which comes to us in so many varieties, sizes, textures, flavors, and colors.

Sandra L. Stewart

Morgan Hill's Mushroom Mardi Gras

*T*his cookbook transports Morgan Hill's Mushroom Mardi Gras into kitchens everywhere. Every spring at Nelson Park, under the watchful eye of Mount El Toro, over thirty-five thousand local residents and visitors celebrate the harvest of mushrooms. In the country air, a spirit of pride mingles with the heady aroma of mushrooms.

The people of Morgan Hill value their rural identity. This small, historical city enjoys a setting that encompasses rich agricultural lowlands bordered by Santa Cruz Mountain and coastal range wilderness. Wineries and farms grace the verdant hills and quiet country roads. When you drive through the area, it's easy to spot the green crops, the grape vines, and the barns and animals. But next time you tour, look also for less conventional farms. Mushrooms do not grow in fields. They are carefully cultivated in-doors. You may see clusters of low-lying buildings, mounds of straw steaming in the balmy air, and signs offering mushroom compost for sale. Inside one of the low-lying, secretive buildings on each of these farms, rows and rows of beautiful mushrooms are just waiting to be picked.

In fact, what makes the Mardi Gras unique among festivals and fairs is its focus on cultivated mushrooms. During the Mardi Gras, the city pays tribute to one of the region's most bountiful year-round crops. The mushrooms that come from these area farms grace the shelves of United States' markets and transform the character of American cooking. The Mardi Gras also caters to those of us who prefer to collect fungi from markets that purchase several cultivated varieties from mushroom farms. The most widely available are the white and brown button mushrooms, Oyster mushrooms, and the Shiitake. Growing and marketing fresh, clean mushrooms is a fascinating art and science explained later in this book.

The Mardi Gras is a time to publicly acknowledge local farmers' ingenuity and considerable contribution to the economy of Morgan Hill. The first Mardi Gras was held thirteen years ago. The founders of the festival wished to blend the celebration of the mushroom harvest with community needs. Their vision anticipated that the yearly Mardi Gras would provide more commerce for local businesses, an awakening of cultural unity, and especially, a focus on the education of Morgan Hill's young people.

At the Mardi Gras, you will see this vision become a reality. Local businesses and civic organizations set up kiosks to provide festive, local food and wine at low prices. You will have a chance to appreciate the delightful performance of community clubs. You will have the choice to enjoy country arts such as trick riding, bluegrass music, and skits of the old West.

Your children can join in the Mardi Gras spirit by dressing up in costumes for the costume parade and contest, and there's more—top name rock-'n-roll and jazz bands and booths full of crafts from all over the country. You will notice that almost everyone in the community gets involved in this yearly event. Mushroom growers, civic leaders, artists, performers, and high school students work side by side.

The people of Morgan Hill value the education of their children. Perhaps the most important difference between the Mardi Gras and other festivals is its emphasis and support of education. Each year, a significant portion of Mardi Gras profits are invested in scholarships for high school graduates. The harvest of children's futures was of great importance to Mardi Gras founders and shines as a continuing tradition of this annual Memorial Day celebration.

Memento

Shaded near a stream, the
    Red Alder, a limbless, dead
        Sentinel, grows shelves of
        creamy Oyster mushrooms, a
    stair-step lattice
    cool as marble.

Never found where sought,
    Mushrooms are silent
        Gifts of the forest that
    distill the wildwood's crumbling feast,
    mementos of the sun.

They issue galaxies of spores and
    climb the tattered trunk,
    white headstones to
    mourn the tree.

R. Timothy Haley

Wild Mushrooms

Cultivated Mushrooms
(Agaricus bisporus)

Farming Mushrooms

*H*eading for the woods with baskets in hand has long been a delightful occupation for wild mushroom lovers around the world. Mushroom farms may seem less romantic, but they are almost as mysterious as the mushroom itself. On California's central coast, the farms are clusters of windowless, low-lying buildings. However, if you dare, shine a light in the harvesting room of any mushroom farm and you will be enchanted by the glistening, white mushrooms growing in thick layers like fairy tale suds in a bathtub.

Mushroom farming is a science and an art. It's complex, high tech agriculture produces large quantities of fresh mushrooms year-round at bargain prices. Just as some chefs are secretive about their best recipes, mushroom growers have their own secret formulas for the "perfect" mushroom crop. In the Morgan Hill area, mushroom farming of the white (*Agaricus bisporus*) variety varies somewhat from farm to farm, but these growers share the same basic principles and processes. Like vegetables, mushrooms are grown in compost, but the similarity ends there. The soil-like material found on store-bought mushrooms is peat moss, a clean layer added to the compost in the fourth phase of the farming process, before harvest. Mushrooms are a fungus that get energy for growth from rich compost, not from sunlight. Mushroom farms, therefore, must provide a cool, dark, indoor environment for growth. Sanitation is of utmost importance to the production of high quality, disease-free mushrooms.

The entire process of growing white button mushrooms takes about two months. There are five phases.

Phase One - Composting (three to five weeks)

Preparing nutrient-rich food for mushrooms is the most important stage in farming. It determines the size and number of mushrooms in a harvest. Common ingredients are straw, water, dried poultry waste, gypsum, and cotton-seed meal. Farmers wet the straw and add the other ingredients. The mixture is repeatedly turned and aerated while being moistened with water, until it is dark and rich with nutrients. The large piles of steaming compost on the mushroom farms reach a temperature of 140 to 170 degrees, killing unwanted spores and bacteria.

Phase Two - Pasteurization (one week)

The farmer moves prepared compost into 4 x 6 inch trays that are nine inches deep, into a sealed, dark room. Clean air is circulated, and then the compost is heated even further to rid it of all impurities.

Phase Three - The Spawn Run (two weeks)

To ensure complete sanitation, the trays are moved to a second sealed room. Here, the finished compost is inoculated with spore (the powdery material that comes from the gills of mushrooms) called "spawn." Special laboratories have prepared the spawn, a rye grain with mushroom mycelium growing in and over it. Mycelium is a white, web-like substance that is similar to the roots of plants. Eating the nutrients in the compost for energy, the mushroom mycelium grows throughout the compost.

Phase Four - Casing and Flushing (two weeks)

The trays of mycelium-rich compost are covered with peat moss, also called "casing soil," which acts as a sponge, holding water for the growth of the mushrooms. The room is flushed with cool, fresh air, which shocks the mycelium into reproducing. Small nodules or "pins" form on the surface of the peat moss. The oxygen from the flushing causes the pins to develop into mushrooms.

Phase Five - Picking (three weeks)

Typically, a farmer flushes and picks from the same crop of mycelium three times. When the pins become mushrooms, they double in size every day. Mushrooms are hand picked according to their maturity, the shape of the cap, and the ratio of the cap to the stem. Every day the pickers harvest the mushrooms that are ready (a certain size and maturity). First, a number of small mushrooms are picked; next, the medium sized ones are picked; and finally, the large mushrooms are picked. (Some farms pick a fourth "jumbo" size.) The crop of mycelium is flushed and picked two more times. When the yield of mushrooms decreases, the crop is sterilized to prevent the spreading of spores and flies. The "spent" compost is then dumped and sold, to be recycled for use in other kinds of farming.

The conditions must be perfect for each kind of mushroom. Even though brown (Crimini) mushrooms are the same variety as white ones, they must be grown separately because they require different temperatures and less water. In Watsonville, California, the farmers of Oyster and Shiitake mushrooms are especially shy about divulging farming methods which have been handed down in Asian families just as the formulas for fine wine are carefully guarded by the French and Italians. Unlike brown and white mushrooms, Oyster and Shiitake mushrooms are, generally, grown out of large balls of special compost, held together with plastic mesh.

The whole process of farming a crop of mushrooms requires precision, controlled temperatures, and scrupulous sanitation. The advantage of such attention means that you and I can enjoy the same high yield and quality of mushrooms year-round. In fact, to ensure maximum freshness, mushrooms are harvested, packed, and shipped on the same day.

Thanks to the knowledge and ingenuity of mushroom farmers, we can serve fresh, cultivated mushrooms in any season.

Eating Mushrooms

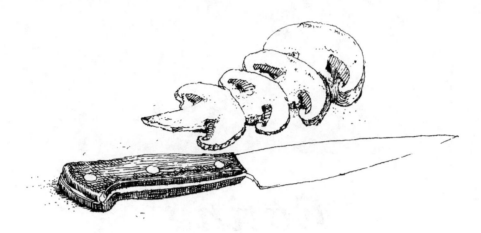

Nutrition

T he nutritional value of the mushroom remains a controversial subject. However, the latest studies show that the mushroom is, indeed, a viable food source. Mushrooms are low in calories and high in roughage. About 90 percent of a mushroom's weight is water. The major food value of mushrooms lies in their protein component. They are high in potassium and niacin, the B2 vitamins. And, when combined with grains, they provide a complete protein. In fact, mushrooms have 0.32 mg. of vitamins per typical serving, and only 20 calories per cup of sliced or diced raw mushrooms.

These days, the consensus among nutritionists and health care advocates is that most of us eat too much protein, especially animal protein, which is high in fat. The average North American eats 100 gm. of protein daily, twice the actual requirement. Not only do mushrooms provide an alternate source of protein, they have minerals such as potassium and magnesium; yet, they are low in sodium. Try reducing the amount of meat in your recipes and adding mushrooms. Or, if you are a vegetarian, mushrooms combined with grains will help satisfy your body's need for protein.

Buying Fresh Mushrooms

*T*hese days, the potential market for mushrooms is so great that large-scale cultivation of an increasing variety offers year-round pleasure. Now, fungus fanciers can do their foraging safely in their favorite supermarkets and specialty stores.

There is no waste in fresh mushrooms sold by the pound. Choose types and sizes according to the use for which they are intended. White button mushrooms sell in four sizes: small, medium, large, and jumbo. Because their size requires special handling by both farmers and cooks, jumbo mushrooms are rarely available in the markets. Jumbo and large mushrooms are excellent for stuffing, or serving as a main dish. Medium-sized mushrooms are good for slicing and sautéing, broiling, barbecuing, or serving whole in casseroles. The small, crisp mushrooms are best for appetizers, sauces, salads, and recipes calling for chopped mushrooms. Brown mushrooms sell mainly in medium or large sizes.

Generally speaking, the white and brown mushrooms grown on North American farms are sold with a closed veil (the membrane between the cap and stem), signifying their freshness. However, don't overlook mushrooms grown to maturity; their veil is open, revealing dark gills. These fresh, open mushrooms are referred to as "matures." You won't see these very often in stores. Farmers usually reserve most of this part of their harvest for pizza chain restaurants. Mature mushrooms are dryer and have more flavor. They are better for stews and sauces, especially Italian. Closed mushrooms contain more liquid and may make your sauces watery and your bread soggy. Also, a stored mushroom that sets on the refrigerator shelf will open and grow. This in no way affects the quality of the mushroom. As long as it looks appealing and fresh, not rotten, it is a good mushroom.

Carefully check mushrooms for freshness. Look for signs of decay—brown, shiny soft spots. Don't be afraid to smell a mushroom before you buy it. A pleasing, earthy, or woodsy aroma means they are fresh. A lack of odor indicates some loss of flavor intensity (possibly the mushroom has been refrigerated for some time). If any mushroom has an unpleasant odor, don't buy it.

Many markets offer a wide variety of both cultivated and wild mushrooms. Experiment with wild varieties carefully. When in doubt, ask the produce buyer whether the mushrooms are cultivated or bought from collectors. At the present time, anyone may collect mushrooms and sell them to retail outlets without a license. Unless there's good reason to trust the produce buyer, who relies mostly on the collector's identification of mushrooms, avoid wild, collected mushrooms.

Many varieties of delicious mushrooms grow wild in the United States, just as they do in other parts of the world. Mushroom hunting is great fun. But, unless you are well-tutored in the subject of mycology (the study of mushrooms) and have plenty of practice discerning which mushrooms are safe and edible, you should not eat wild mushrooms that you gather. Just enjoy their amazing diversity of scent, shape, and color.

Limiting yourself to cultivated varieties does not mean mushroom deprivation. Far from it. The ambitious mushroom cook can count on consistent, milder flavors from the versatile white mushroom, a more robust taste from the brown mushroom, and subtle textures combined with much more varied flavors from cultivated Oyster and Shiitake specimens. And, as farmers learn about other, more exotic mushrooms, we can look forward to new cultivated species on our market shelves.

For new culinary adventures, expand your mushroom repertoire. Brown mushrooms, though not as widely available as white, have a big, deep flavor and a tougher skin, which allows them a slightly longer shelf life than the white mushrooms.

Oyster mushrooms are more expensive than the white and brown variety. The creamy tan to light pink color and shell-like shape of the Oyster makes it easily one of the most decorative of all mushrooms. The Oyster is quite fragile. Unfortunately, these mushrooms are often old or roughly treated in markets; it is difficult to imagine their striking beauty. Always choose firm, young specimens since Oyster mushrooms toughen as they mature.

Even more costly are the Shiitake. The word means, literally, "oak mushroom." When fresh, they have narrow, whitish stems and rich, pecan-brown caps which curl under around the edges. Fresh Shiitake have become more available, but you may have an easier time finding dry ones (almost all Chinese and Japanese markets sell them). There are many grades and prices of dried Shiitake. Shop with care. Buy the thick, *donko* types if you can find them. These have thick flesh, and the caps are only partly opened. In Asian cultures, the *donko* is considered medicinally superior. They are expensive but well worth the price when reconstituted. Their flavor is robust and their texture meaty, allowing the Shiitake mushroom to serve as a primary ingredient, or successfully enhance stronger-flavored foods.

Don't hesitate. Put mushrooms to the taste test before investing time and money. Buy one mushroom of a tempting variety. Slice and sauté a small piece in butter or oil until it is soft. Eat it with plain crackers or toast to determine whether the flavor quality and intensity appeals to you. Think about how you might use it in a recipe.

Shopping for mushrooms is an adventure. Enjoy the beautiful eye-catching displays in your markets. Don't pass them by. Let mushrooms add the joy of sensory details to your home cooking. The rewards are worth the effort.

Storing Mushrooms

Store fresh mushrooms, unwashed, in the refrigerator. If, when you buy them, they are well packaged (without any cellophane or plastic), keep them in the original containers. If only plastic bags are available at your supermarket, immediately transfer your mushrooms to waxed or brown paper bags at home. Water condenses on plastic bags; too much moisture makes mushrooms soggy. If they are already moist when you buy them, put the mushrooms in a bowl lined and covered with a cloth or paper towel before refrigerating.

As a rule, white mushrooms can be stored for up to a week, depending on their freshness, packaging, and your refrigerator's storage temperature. Brown mushrooms have an even longer shelf life, up to eight or nine days. Because of their delicacy, Oyster mushrooms should be eaten within three to four days. Fresh Shiitake are best eaten within one or two days of purchase.

Let each type of mushroom guide your creativity. To get the best from your stock of fresh mushrooms, display the crisp, younger white or Oyster mushrooms in appetizers, soups, and salads. Enjoy larger, older, or mature mushrooms sautéed, broiled, barbecued, or in rich Italian sauces, stews, steam pots, casseroles, and on pizzas. Since they are more expensive and perish more quickly, carefully plan meals featuring fresh Oyster or Shiitake and buy only what is needed to fill the requirements of each recipe.

Cleaning and Preparing Mushrooms

C lean mushrooms just before you use them. Cultivated mushrooms sold in markets are exquisitely clean. Sometimes flecks of sterile peat moss may cling to their caps and stems. Be aware that mushrooms sold loose in bins are handled more and may need slightly more cleaning. Most mushroom cooks agree, however, that too much washing may destroy the flavor and composition of the mushroom. Avoid streaming water from faucets, especially on the undersides of open caps. Avoid soaking or boiling; your mushrooms will bloat with unnecessary liquid and lose much of their flavor.

The best way to rid mushrooms of any surface debris is to use a soft, damp cloth to wipe each cap and stem and then dry them immediately. For occasions when large amounts of mushrooms are needed, using the damp-cloth method may be slow and tedious. A helpful tip for cleaning large numbers of white or brown mushrooms was passed along to workers at Morgan Hill's Mushroom Mardi Gras by John Sorci, Bon Appetít Square's famous chef: Fill the sink. Put in the mushrooms. Sprinkle cornstarch over the mushrooms. Swirl the water. Remove the mushrooms and drain. It works. Not only are the mushrooms clean; they have a new, whiter sparkle.

Allow at least half an hour drying time for mushrooms that have been totally immersed in water. To speed up the drying time, carefully toss mushrooms in a dry, hot skillet for a minute or two before preparing them.

Preparation

Cultivated mushrooms do not need to be peeled. If the stems are hard and discolored, trim away the dry, woody parts. Reserve the stems; some recipes call for them to be removed and used separately as part of the sauce. Stems can be added to vegetable or chicken stock, as well. The very fresh white and brown mushrooms need little preparation. Eat them whole with dips or sliced in salads. The pieces are beautiful when sliced, and they are more chewy when quartered. To keep sliced mushrooms from becoming discolored, sprinkle them with lemon juice. White or brown mushrooms are best sliced before they are cooked, allowing for more rapid cooking and also more broth.

A sharp 5-inch paring knife is the best tool for slicing mushrooms. Cut them into uniform pieces so they will cook more evenly. For perfectly matched slices, try an egg slicer. Trim the stem and place the mushroom, cap facing downward, into the slicer.

As mushroom cooks and co-authors of this book, for our taste, mushrooms are generally sliced much too thinly in American recipes for appetizers, casseroles, stews, and Italian sauces. Whole mushrooms and large, thick slices or irregular pieces provide more enjoyment, more savory juice and chewy texture per bite. This choice falls in line with our preference for the art of home cooking with its emphasis on whole foods. We say, don't hide your mushrooms by slashing them into measly bits; liberate them! Be proud to expose their raw, natural beauty as a main characteristic of your soups and sauces. Let the range of choices in your home cooking reveal the mushroom's capacity to be humble and elegant at the same time.

Oyster mushrooms are thinner and more brittle than white and brown mushrooms. They should be handled gently. The Oyster needs little cleaning. Use a damp cloth, sparingly. Cut off the lower part of the stems; they are tough, so discard them. Since the caps are thin and cook quickly, do not slice Oyster mushrooms. Simply tear them into desired sizes before cooking. They can be dried, but they are better fresh. If you do use dried Oyster mushrooms, there is no need to reconstitute them (soak in hot water) before cooking. Add the dry caps directly to your recipe.

Shiitake mushrooms sell fresh or dried. Since the dried ones have a more concentrated flavor and can be stored for a long time, most cooks prefer them. To prepare dried Shiitake, soak the smaller ones or those cut into pieces for about thirty minutes. If the mushrooms are large and whole, soak them for up to two or three hours; then drain (save the soaking liquid to add back to your dish or put into stock for some other meal). Cut the leathery stems off both the fresh and soaked dried Shiitake. To take full advantage of its beauty and taste, slice the large, fresh Shiitake in quarters before cooking it. Slice the smaller, fresh Shiitake in half so that it will lie flat on the surface of the cutting board.

Measurements

When you measure mushrooms for cooking, remember this principle: A pound of raw mushrooms yields about four cups of chopped pieces or six cups of slices, but will reduce to about a third of those amounts when cooked.

To estimate the number of mushrooms to buy, follow these guidelines:

- 1 lb. = 40-55 small mushrooms

- 1 lb. = 20-39 medium mushrooms

- 1 lb. = 15-19 large mushrooms

Cooking Tips

O f the four kinds of mushrooms discussed in this book, only the white and brown button mushrooms can be eaten raw. Oyster and Shiitake mushrooms are more nutritious and digestible cooked. Cooking intensifies the distinctive flavor of any mushroom. To get the most from cooking mushrooms, we suggest:

- Avoid overcooking. In stews, soups, and casseroles, mushrooms break down quickly, especially if these dishes set on the stove or counter before being served. Today, mushrooms are "coming out of the closet." Think of the full-bodied flavor of mushrooms as a central ingredient in your recipe, not a mushy afterthought. While dried mushrooms will stand more cooking, fresh mushrooms fare best when added to hot pans or baked dishes only seven to ten minutes before serving. The mushrooms will then be at their tastiest, just starting to burst with fragrant, delicious liquid and plump up with chewy texture.

- Enhance the subtle flavor of mushrooms with unsaturated oil instead of whole butter or rich cream whenever possible, or try using smaller amounts of oil, butter and cream, taking advantage of the mushroom's natural juices. Allow the mushroom, a low-calorie, nutritious whole food, to lead the other ingredients in your recipe, not just follow them.

- Try the mushroom as your main ingredient. White, brown, and Shiitake varieties have a dense, chewy quality. In China and Japan, mushrooms are often used as the central ingredient in main dishes. They can be teamed with almost any vegetable and grain for a lighter, low-fat, nutritious meal. They are right for today's health-conscious cooks and their families.

Two Methods for Sautéing Mushrooms

- Sauté thick-sliced mushrooms in a small amount of butter or oil over medium heat. Lightly stir-fry them for five to seven minutes until they are crisp-tender and have begun to "sweat," releasing broth.

- For an intensified flavor, dry-sauté thinly-sliced mushrooms. Heat a non-stick skillet or wok on medium-high and add the oil or butter. When oil is hot, stir in the mushrooms. Continue stir-frying them for about ten minutes or until they have reabsorbed all the liquid in the pan.

Preserving Mushrooms

Fresh, cultivated mushrooms are now widely available, but there are several reasons for preserving them for later use.

- The Oyster and Shiitake varieties perish more quickly than most fruits and vegetables, and they are more expensive than white and brown mushrooms.

- Many markets do not carry a regular supply of all four types of cultivated mushroom. Stores convenient for you may have "a run" on a certain kind of mushroom and then be unable to get it again for several months. Consider buying a larger supply and preserving part of your purchase.

- The drying process intensifies the flavor of some kinds of mushrooms; for instance, dried Shiitake have a much stronger, more distinctive flavor than fresh ones.

- Preserved mushrooms shorten the preparation time of meals. Make stocks, sauces, and sautéed mushrooms in advance and freeze them, to save time and ensure authentic mushroom flavor and texture in your more complicated, time-consuming recipes. Whole mushrooms and condiments such as mushroom relish can be frozen, as well. For a handy pungent seasoning, dried mushrooms can be powdered and stored in tightly-covered containers.

Drying

An age-old method of preserving food, drying is still a good way to keep mushrooms on hand for a long time, unspoiled. However, mushrooms must be thoroughly dry before you store them. Otherwise, they will begin to mold and decay. Be sure to use specimens that are in great shape. Clean the mushrooms with little or no water, since, in drying, you want to eliminate all moisture.

You can choose from a number of methods for drying. In warm weather, the mushrooms can be sliced into thin, broad, uniform pieces and placed on screens or trays to dry. Sun dry the mushrooms by laying them in a single layer on a cookie sheet or tray lined with several layers of paper towels. Turn the slices occasionally, and if they are not dry by sundown, bring them indoors. Repeat the process daily until the mushrooms are as brittle and dry as thin tree bark.

In wet weather, dry mushrooms indoors. Spread the slices on a cookie sheet and put them in a warm (less than 100 degree) oven. Circulation is more important than heat; you want moisture to be carried away. Spread the mushroom slices on screens and heat them under a warm, bright light bulb. Try a hot plate, or, if possible, buy a dehydrator. Better yet, use the heat above an oven, fireplace, or heater. With wire or cord, hang flats of wire screen doors or plastic mesh above your heat source.

Store your dried mushrooms in well-sealed jars, out of the sunlight. They provide a colorful, homey addition to your kitchen, and jars of aromatic, convenient "mushroom chips" make easy, interesting gifts. Dried mushrooms stored in jars should last from four to six months before their essence begins to fade.

For the most natural and enchanting effect, make a garland of whole mushrooms. Use heavy carpet-mending thread and a large needle. Pull the thread through the stems of the mushrooms, leaving the caps intact. Leave space between the mushrooms for air to circulate; then hang the garland over a warm oven or in a sunny corner to dry. Your kitchen will be as fragrant and folksy as the stalls in Polish or Russian markets, where the practice of stringing mushroom garlands originated hundreds of years ago.

Freezing

Another good way of preserving mushrooms is to freeze them, raw or precooked. Whole, raw mushrooms should be firm and fresh. Clean them and let them dry for twenty to thirty minutes. Freeze them in a single, uncovered layer until they are solid, and then pack the frozen mushrooms into heavy plastic bags or freezer containers. Whole mushrooms frozen raw should be eaten within one month.

For parties, try the whole-frozen method to prepare stuffed, uncooked mushrooms in advance. Stuff the raw mushrooms according to your recipe instructions. Freeze them in a single, uncovered layer. Pack them carefully in a sealed box or a plastic freezer container. Later, before the party or meal, transfer the frozen, stuffed mushrooms to cookie sheets and bake them at the prescribed temperature. The actual baking time may be longer for frozen, stuffed mushrooms than that suggested by your recipe, so check the baking mushrooms more often.

The best way to freeze mushrooms is to cook them first:

- Sauté the mushrooms in butter or oil and one or two tablespoons of lemon juice for five minutes. Put the cooled mushrooms, liquid included, into sealed freezer containers. The French call this fragrant, convenient mixture *Duxelles*.

- Freeze a prepared mushroom dish. Completely cool the food, such as quiche, lasagne, or casserole, and seal it in a freezer container.

Precooked, frozen mushrooms will store well for up to six months.

Preserving mushrooms whole or as an ingredient with other foods will expand your mushroom-cooking opportunities and make cooking more convenient. Keep dried mushrooms on your kitchen shelf or delicious sautéed mushrooms in your freezer, ready to add a special, elegant touch to any recipe.

Wine and Mushrooms

*T*he first rule of wine drinking, in general, and wine drinking with mushrooms, in particular, is that there are no rules. While fresh Ahi tuna and dried Shiitake mushrooms are as well suited to each other as white wine and cheese, countless food and wine combinations have never been tried.

Wine selection is an art, not a science. A recipe is a plan of action which should be followed. That is, unless you as the cook, have an intuition. Act on it; you may have created a work of art. I suggest that when you combine something outstanding, write it down. What you did in the heat of cooking is as fleeting as a dream and just as precious. You are recording the footsteps of the wine in its mysterious dance with the mushroom of your choice.

Both the wine and the mushroom live, breathe, and change, independent of the ingredients in your recipe. For fun and enlightenment, taste various wines with an array of lightly sautéed fresh mushrooms. Eat them with crackers. Compare and contrast the mushroom varieties first without wines, and then with them. (In our home, we call this event the "Shoot-out-at-the Lazy-Susan" Mushroom and Wine Tasting.)

You may have noticed that wines are part of many recipes in this book. For cooking, choosing the best wine to complement a mushroom depends on all the ingredients and how they come together. The alchemical properties of your choice by no means guarantee a certain taste when you're mixing wine and mushrooms with other ingredients. Remember that wine, like mushrooms, is always added at the end of the cooking cycle; alcohol evaporates quickly. The recipes in this book reflect the popular choice of dry sherry (a fortified wine) to accompany white or brown mushrooms. Other choices are brandy (a distillation of wine) and, of course, red and white wines. For mushroom cookery, keep inexpensive bottles of dry sherry and brandy, and cheap bottles of jug red and white wines in a cabinet near your stove top. There is no need to cook with expensive, vibrant wines. Save them for the table.

It's only natural to serve wines with a mushroomy brunch or main meal. This essay cannot cover all the choices. A complete investigation would require a world tour. Sadly, I must skip the rudiments of *haute cuisine*, the brilliant vintage French vines which date back to Roman times, and the two dozen cultivated mushroom varieties that grow in deep caves in France. I haven't time to cover the Portuguese port wines or the choice food and wine districts of Italy. You and I cannot take a trip up the Rhine (except for one quick tip about German whites. If *Mosel* is on the label, it's probably a better wine.).

Since this essay is only an introduction, you will have to continue your wine tour without me. My taste leans toward American wines because they are so easily available and usually less expensive. This essay concentrates on choosing wines to accompany the four main cultivated mushrooms grown in the United States.

The white mushroom (*Agaricus bisporus*) is often served with light or neutral foods such as cheese, fresh vegetables, or fish. I recommend that you "stay light." Stick to delicate, sweet, or mildly dry white wines such as a *Johannisberg Riesling* or *Muscat Canelli*. A *Fumé Blanc* is dryer.

For some recipes, the choice or necessity may be white mushrooms, but the resulting dishes deepen in complexity, texture, or spiciness. I think you should still stick to white wine. For instance, the wine should match the complexity of our "Louisiana Grits Soufflé with Mushroom-Creole Sauce" with the dryness of a versatile larger-style *Fumé Blanc*. A succulent *Chardonnay* should enhance a heavier fish recipe such as Monterey Mushrooms' "Shrimp Creole."

Although the same species as the white, the brown mushroom has a darker, richly-complex flavor which changes the style and essence of a dish. Although whites and browns are listed as if they are interchangeable in many recipes in this book, they are very different mushrooms. Browns go well in heavier, spicier dishes.

Some of the full-bodied red wines will serve, not just as a complement, but as a catalyst that awakens deeper flavors and aromas in mushrooms. For example, if instead of white, you choose brown mushrooms for the "Louisiana Grits Soufflé," consider switching from a dry white to a red, spicy wine such as *Zinfandel* or *Petite Sirah*. The brown mushroom may be improved, as well, by lighter reds such as *Pinot Noir* and *Gamay Beaujolais*. For savory brown mushroom dishes with rich sauces such as our "Brown Mushroom, Eggplant, and Caper Lasagne," choose red wines with depth, including *Zinfandel*, *Barbera*, *Cabernet Sauvignon*, and the less expensive but equally hearty Spanish, Australian, and Chilean red wines.

Our friend Connie Hill's wonderfully gamy "Roast Venison with Mushrooms" goes best with brown mushrooms and a *Zinfandel*. With either whites or browns, wild game, red meats, and decisively-spiced vegetables call for the heavy artillery of aged and oaked *Cabernet Sauvignon* and *Zinfandel* (serve it cooler than California "room temperature." Try the *Zinfandel* as cold as the frosty whites).

The Oyster mushroom is more than decorative. It has a damp, foresty, sweet-grass aroma and is even slightly smoky, when fresh. Try a sweet, white wine such as the smoky *Gewurztraminer*.

Of all four commercially grown mushrooms, the Shiitake has the most aromatically-complex, full-bodied flavor. The most pungent Shiitake mushrooms are the many dried varieties. Choices of wines are implied by the ingredients in the recipe. The Shiitake has such a lively oak or chaparral taste that *Zinfandel*, *Barbera*, or other spicy wines tease out the unique essence of this mushroom species.

Challenge yourself, the cook, to be an artist. You can create your own wonderful meals. Play with the variety and amount of mushrooms and then reverse course by pouring a brilliant wine no one would have thought possible. These are the best meals, filled with surprises. The wisest cooks conjure up secret, subtle nuances, often inspirationally, on the spot.

R. Timothy Haley

Mushroom Recipes

The mushroom craze is new in America, but in most parts of the world the subtle flavors and the aromas of esculent fungi have delighted gourmets from time immemorial.

Kings of ancient Babylon dined on quince-sized truffles from the African deserts, and one mushroom (the Amenita caesarea) pleased the Roman emperors so much that they named it the Imperial Fungus.

Historians still argue whether it was Caligua or Emperor Claudius who proclaimed mushrooms "Food for the gods," too good for common folks.

Margaret Leibenstein, *The Edible Mushroom: a Gourmet Guide*

Appetizers

Capital Stuffed Mushrooms

Penny Lockhart, Favorite Recipe Contest Finalist,
Morgan Hill's Mushroom Mardi Gras

An original, Central California Coast creation. Mushrooms, garlic, and artichokes team up for a gastronomic celebration of Morgan Hill's Mushroom Mardi Gras, Gilroy's Garlic Festival, and Castro Valley's Artichoke Festival.

2 lb. fresh large, white or brown mushrooms

2 tbsp. butter

½ cup finely chopped green onions

4 cloves finely chopped garlic

1 cup fresh bread crumbs (preferably French bread)

1 cup fresh Parmesan cheese, finely grated

½ cup cream or evaporated milk

Juice of ½ lemon

½ of a 6 oz. jar of marinated artichoke hearts, finely chopped, plus marinating liquid from the jar

With a small paring knife, remove stems from mushrooms. Finely chop stems. In a large saucepan, melt butter and sauté stems, onions, and garlic over low heat for 7 minutes. Remove from heat. Stir in bread crumbs.

Place open mushroom caps on a foil-lined cookie sheet.

In blender, on low speed, combine cheese, cream or milk, and lemon juice. Add to mushroom mixture, along with chopped artichoke hearts and marinating liquid from jar. Mix thoroughly.

Salt and pepper to taste. Fill the mushroom caps with mushroom-artichoke mixture, rounding the tops. Cover with foil and bake at 350 degrees for 10 minutes.

Serve hot. Serves 10-12.

Onion Dip with Mushrooms

Courtesy of Monterey Mushrooms, Santa Cruz, California

A mellow onion dip just right with fresh mushrooms. 194 calories per cup.

2 beef bouillon cubes

1 container (8 oz.) plain lowfat yogurt

¼ tsp. sugar

2 tbsp. instant toasted onions

Fresh large white mushrooms, thickly sliced

In a decorative bowl, break up bouillon cubes. Stir in yogurt, onion, and sugar. Cover. Chill at least 4 hours to blend flavors. Stir, serve with mushrooms slices. Makes about 1 cup.

Mushroom and Spinach Dip

Anita M. Sing

A favorite party-pleaser with a new twist.

1 pkg. dried vegetable soup mix

1½ cups sour cream

1 cup mayonnaise

1 pkg. (10 oz.) chopped frozen spinach, thawed and squeezed dry

1 can (8 oz.) water chestnuts, chopped

½ cup green onions, chopped

2 cups fresh large white mushrooms (1½ cups chopped, ½ cup thinly sliced)

1 large round loaf sourdough bread

1 baguette sourdough bread

In a large bowl, combine soup mix, sour cream, and mayonnaise until blended. Stir in spinach, water chestnuts, green onions, and chopped mushrooms. Cover bowl and chill for at least 2 hours. Hollow out sourdough round loaf and spoon dip into "bread bowl." Garnish with sliced mushrooms. Slice spooned out sourdough bread and baguette; serve on a plate next to dip. When dip is gone, cut up bread bowl and serve. Serves 10-12.

Mushroom Caponata

Sandra L. Stewart and R. Timothy Haley

Caponata is an antipasto made from fresh vegetables. Serve it hot or cold, with crackers or pita bread. Store left-over Caponata in the refrigerator or freezer for subsequent use. Makes about 6 cups.

½ cup pine nuts

1 medium eggplant, unpeeled

2 red or green bell peppers cut in 1-inch pieces

2½ lb. tomatoes, peeled, seeded, and diced (or 1 can (28 oz.) Italian plum tomatoes, chopped)

1½ cups celery, cut in ½ inch slices

2 cloves garlic, chopped

¾ cup stuffed green olives, sliced

½ cup parsley, chopped

¼ cup fresh basil, chopped, (or 2 tbsp. dried basil)

⅔ cup red wine vinegar

2 tbsp. tomato paste

2 tbsp. sugar

1 tsp. freshly ground black pepper

2 carrots, thinly sliced

2 zucchini, thinly sliced

1 lb. fresh white or brown mushrooms, thickly sliced

Lightly toast the pine nuts in an 8-inch frying pan over medium heat; set aside. Cut the unpeeled eggplant into 1-inch cubes. Place the cubes in a 5 or 6-quart casserole or Dutch oven. Add the pine nuts and the remaining ingredients, except for the mushrooms, and stir gently. Bring to a boil. Reduce the heat to low. Cover the casserole or Dutch oven and simmer slowly for 30 minutes. Add the mushroom slices. Stir Caponata occasionally while it simmers, uncovered, for about 10 minutes longer, or until thickened. Serves 14-16.

Mushrooms Florentine

Mrs. Paul Eilert, Favorite Recipe Contest,
Morgan Hill's Mushroom Mardi Gras

A classic Italian appetizer that evokes images of the architecture and sculpture of Florence, Italy. For full effect, follow up with a green salad, pasta main dish, crusty bread, and a bottle of Pinot Noir wine. Listen to an Italian opera while you cook and eat.

12 large white or brown mushrooms

¼ cup butter

1 onion, minced

2 cloves garlic, minced

1 pkg. (10 oz.) spinach, defrosted
  and chopped

1 egg yolk

5 tbsp. Parmesan cheese

⅛ tsp. pepper

⅛ tsp. salt

⅛ tsp. nutmeg

With a small paring knife, carefully remove stems from mushrooms. Finely chop the stems and set aside. In a saucepan, melt butter. Pour half the melted butter into a large baking dish. Turn caps over in butter and arrange cut side up in baking dish.

Add chopped stems, onions, and garlic to remaining butter. Sauté till soft; remove from heat. Squeeze spinach dry. Stir in spinach, egg yolk, pepper, salt, nutmeg, and half the Parmesan cheese. Fill caps. Sprinkle with remaining cheese. Bake at 325 degrees for 15 minutes. If made ahead of time, bake chilled mushrooms for 20-25 minutes. Serves 6-8.

William's Marinated Mushrooms

William J. Vette, Favorite Recipe Contest,
Morgan Hill's Mushroom Mardi Gras

This spicy version livens up any party or serves as a light antipasto before an Italian meal.

4 cups water

1 lb. fresh small white mushroom caps
(stems cut flush with bottom of each cap)

½ c. white wine vinegar

⅛ tsp. ground coriander seed

2 tsp. whole coriander seed

1 tsp. mustard seed

⅛ tsp. ground cinnamon

2 bay leaves, crumbled

3 cloves garlic, peeled and quartered

3 small red peppers, cut in strips

3 tbsp. olive oil

Safflower, sunflower, or peanut oil to fill jars.

Wash and sterilize 3 half-pint jars.

Bring water to a boil in 3 or 4-quart saucepan. Add mushrooms; boil for 1½ minutes after water resumes boiling. Drain. Set mushrooms aside. Reserve ½ cup of the liquid. (Balance of the liquid may be used for making soup or stock.)

In small saucepan, combine vinegar, coriander seed, mustard seed, cinnamon, and bay leaves. Boil on medium-high for 6 minutes.

Divide the mushrooms equally between the three sterilized jars. Add 4 quarters of garlic and a third of the pepper strips to each jar. Pour spiced liquid, equally divided, into jars. Allowing ½ inch headspace, add 1 tablespoon olive oil to each jar, and fill with either a safflower, sunflower, or peanut oil. Seal with air-tight lids.

Allow at least one week in the refrigerator for full flavor to develop; flavor will be improved if the jars are frequently shaken while stored. Bottled mushrooms will keep, refrigerated, for up to 4 weeks. Serves 12.

Crab Stuffed Mushrooms

Jan Trimble, Favorite Recipe Contest Finalist,
Morgan Hill's Mushroom Mardi Gras

These two delicacies are meant for each other.

12 large or 18 medium mushrooms

¼ cup salad oil

7 or 8 oz. fresh cooked crab meat,
  flaked
  (or 1 can (7½ oz.) crab meat

1 egg, lightly beaten

2 tbsp. mayonnaise

2 tbsp. onion, finely chopped

1 tsp. lemon juice

½ cup soft bread crumbs

2 tbsp. butter or margarine

Remove stems from mushrooms (save stems for use in soups or sauces). Brush mushroom caps with oil and place in buttered baking dish. In a mixing bowl, combine crab meat, egg, mayonnaise, onion, lemon juice, and ¼ cup bread crumbs. Fill the mushroom caps with mixture. Combine remaining ¼ cup bread crumbs with melted butter and sprinkle over crab mixture.

Arrange mushrooms on a foil-lined cookie sheet. Bake in 375 degree oven for 15 minutes. Serve immediately. For more guests double the recipe. Serves 6-8.

Sautéed Mushrooms

Margaret Fortino, Morgan Hill's Mushroom Mardi Gras Cookoff

A simple sauté of artfully-carved mushrooms.

2 lb. fresh small white mushrooms

½ cup butter

1 tbsp. lemon juice

2 tbsp. parsley, finely minced

1 tsp. salt, to taste

½ tsp. freshly ground pepper, to taste

Cut off mushroom stems flush with caps. With a small curved knife, cut grooves that curve out from the center-top of each cap to its edges.

Melt butter in large skillet until hot and foaming. Add mushrooms, with grooved side down. Mix in lemon juice and parsley; sprinkle with salt and pepper. Toss mushrooms gently over high heat about 3 minutes, or until evenly golden. Serves 8.

Mushrooms Stuffed with Butter and Walnuts

Jody Ruff, Morgan Hill's Mushroom Mardi Gras Cookoff

Nuts are an excellent complement to the woodsy flavor of mushrooms.

10-12 fresh medium, white or brown mushrooms

½ lb. sweet butter

4 shallots, finely chopped

2 cloves garlic, finely chopped

5 tbsp. parsley, finely chopped

½ cup walnuts, finely chopped

Salt, to taste

Pepper, to taste

With a small paring knife, remove stems from mushrooms. (Reserve stems for soups or stock.) Lay caps, top side down, in a well-buttered baking dish. Mix butter, shallots, garlic, parsley, and walnuts. Add salt and pepper. Fill mushroom caps. Five minutes before serving, place mushrooms 6 inches from flame under the broiler for 5 or 6 minutes. Serves 4.

Sausage Stuffed Mushrooms
Helen Fritz, Favorite Recipe Contest,
Morgan Hill's Mushroom Mardi Gras

An excellent and filling hors d'oeuvre. Sage and sherry-laced sausage is perfect for mushrooms.

12-14 fresh large, white or brown
  mushrooms

1 lb. lean sausage

1 medium onion, chopped

⅔ cup dry bread crumbs

3 tbsp. Parmesan cheese, grated

¼ tsp. crushed sage

2 tbsp. plus ¼ cup sherry

¼ tsp. salt, to taste

4 tbsp. sweet butter

With small paring knife, remove stems from mushrooms. Finely chop stems and set aside. In large skillet, crush sausage with a fork. Sauté on medium-high heat. When sausage is partially cooked, add onion. When onion is soft, pour off fat. Add chopped mushrooms, bread crumbs, Parmesan cheese, sage, salt, 2 tablespoons of sherry, and cheese. Cook 2 or 3 minutes longer. Arrange mushrooms in large baking dish. Pack stuffing into caps.

In small saucepan, heat 4 tablespoons of butter and ¼ cup sherry. Pour over mushrooms and bake at 350 degrees for 7-10 minutes. Or, cook and serve in a chafing dish on the table. Serves 8-10.

Japanese-Style Stuffed Mushrooms

Ellie Brady, 2nd Place, Favorite Recipe Contest,
Morgan Hill's Mushroom Mardi Gras

Soy sauce, *sake*, and crispy toasted sesame seeds give these mushrooms a distinctly Japanese appearance and flavor.

1 lb. fresh large, white or brown mushrooms

1 lb. extra-lean ground pork

1 small onion, finely chopped

1 small can water chestnuts, chopped

1 large egg, lightly scrambled

1 tbsp. soy sauce

2 tbsp. *sake* or white wine (optional)

1 cup sesame seeds

With a small paring knife, remove stems from mushrooms. Finely chop stems. In a large bowl, combine stems with ground pork, onion, water chestnuts, scrambled egg, soy sauce, and *sake* or wine. Mix well. Stuff mixture into each mushroom cap, forming mound. Dip tops of stuffed mushrooms into small bowl of sesame seeds.

On a cookie sheet, place mushrooms 5 inches from flame in broiler for 8-10 minutes. Serve immediately. Serves 6-8.

Italian Mushrooms

Kathy Sass, Morgan Hill's Mushroom Mardi Gras Cookoff Finalist

A colorful trio of bite-sized delicacies for the party table.

3 Italian sausages, cut in 1 inch lengths

3 cloves garlic, minced

2 lb. fresh medium, white or brown mushrooms, *parboiled and drained

2 cans artichoke hearts (not marinated), quartered

4 tbsp. olive oil

Salt, to taste

Pepper, to taste

2 tbsp. fresh parsley, chopped

To parboil, boil mushrooms until slightly cooked

Line sausage pieces down middle of large oblong baking pan. Put garlic at bottom of pan on both ends. Line mushrooms on one side of pan and artichokes on the other. Drizzle oil over mushrooms and artichokes. Sprinkle salt, pepper, and parsley over all.

Bake covered, at 325 degrees for 30 minutes. Uncover and continue baking an additional 30 minutes. Remove to a serving platter. Serves 10-12.

Stuffed Mushrooms Italienne

Emma Moretti, Favorite Recipe Contest,
Morgan Hill's Mushroom Mardi Gras

Anchovies, vinegar, and garlic infuse ground beef with a rich Italian flavor.

3 dozen medium white or brown
  mushrooms

⅔ cup plus 3 tbsp. butter

1½ lb. extra-lean ground beef

7 anchovy filets, drained and
  chopped

3 cloves garlic, crushed

2 tbsp. parsley, chopped

¼ tsp. red pepper

pinch salt

2 tbsp. water

2 tbsp. olive oil

2 tbsp. red wine vinegar

1 cup dry bread crumbs

With a small paring knife, remove stems from mushrooms. Finely chop stems.

In a large skillet, sauté stems for 5 minutes in ⅔ cup butter. Add the beef, anchovies, garlic, parsley, red pepper, and salt. Combine water and oil in a large baking dish. Arrange mushroom caps in dish, top sides down. Pile caps high with beef mixture. Put a few drops of vinegar on each. Sprinkle with bread crumbs and dot with remaining butter.

Bake at 425 degrees for 15 minutes; then brown mushrooms for 5 minutes, 5 inches from flame in the broiler. Serves 15-18.

Beer and Cheese Stuffed Mushrooms

Linda Tarvin, Morgan Hill's Mushroom Mardi Gras Cookoff

An unusual and tasty combination, just right for a party.

2 lb. fresh medium or large, white or brown mushrooms

2 beef bouillon cubes

$\frac{1}{2}$ cup beer, warmed

2 cups sharp cheddar cheese, grated

$\frac{1}{4}$ cup bleu cheese, crumbled

1 can (2$\frac{1}{4}$ oz.) sliced black olives, drained

2 tbsp. butter, softened

3 cloves garlic, pressed or minced

1 tbsp. soy sauce

$\frac{1}{2}$ tsp. hot pepper sauce

1 tbsp. lemon juice

2 tbsp. fresh parsley, chopped

With a small paring knife, remove stems from mushrooms. (Reserve stems for soups or stock.) Dissolve bouillon cubes in beer.

Combine cheeses, olives, butter, garlic, soy sauce, pepper sauce, lemon juice and parsley. Mix well. Gradually add bouillon-beer mixture. Stuff mushrooms. Place on a foil-covered cookie sheet and bake for 10 minutes at 350 degrees or until filling is bubbly.

Serves 10-12.

Mini Mushroom Tarts

Sharon Leyman, Morgan Hill's Mushroom Mardi Gras Cookoff

Tasty mouthfuls of sour cream pastry and rich, mushroom cream.

Pastry

2½ cups flour

½ tsp. salt

⅔ cup cold butter

1 egg, beaten

⅔ cup sour cream

Filling

¼ cup butter

1 or 2 green onions, tops included, minced

½ lb. white or brown mushrooms, puréed

¼ cup flour

½ tsp. salt

1 cup heavy cream

Pastry

Combine flour and salt in bowl. Cut in butter, using two knives or pastry blender, until particles are pea-sized. Combine egg and sour cream; add to flour mixture. Mix, using hands, if necessary. Form a ball of dough.

Shape dough into ¾-1 inch balls, and press into bottom and up sides of miniature muffin tins (each muffin mold approx. 1 inch across). Dough should be thin. Bake at 400 degrees for 12 minutes, until golden. Cool.

Filling

Melt butter in medium skillet. Add chopped onions and mushrooms. Sauté over medium heat 4 or 5 minutes. Add flour and salt; stir well. Gradually add cream, stirring constantly till sauce is thick, smooth, and bubbling.

Fill baked pastry shells ¾ full. Bake at 400 degrees for 12-15 minutes. Tarts may be baked 1 day before serving, refrigerated, and reheated, or they may be baked and frozen. Defrost 1 hour before reheating.

Makes 48 tarts (Re-use tins for second set of 24). Serves 25-28.

Mushroom Won Ton Appetizers

Judy Cummings, Morgan Hill's Mushroom Mardi Gras Cookoff

Crispy, Chinese treats add variety and mushroom flavor to your buffet.

4 tsp. butter

1 lb. fresh white or brown mushrooms, chopped finely

3 cloves garlic, minced

1 medium onion, minced

Salt, to taste

Pepper, to taste

1 package Won Ton skins

1 egg, beaten

3 cups salad oil

Hot mustard

Catsup

In a large skillet, melt butter. Add mushrooms, garlic, and onion. Cook until all liquid has evaporated. Add salt and pepper.

Mound approximately one teaspoon of filling onto one corner of a Won Ton skin. Roll the skin over the filling and pinch ends together. Moisten corners with beaten egg. In a large skillet, heat about 2 inches of salad oil to 360 degrees. Fry 4-6 Won Ton at a time until golden brown. Turn to cook evenly. Drain. Serve warm with hot mustard and catsup for dipping. Makes 24-26 Won Ton. Serves 12-14.

Paté Stuffed Mushrooms

Loiane Chastek, Morgan Hill's Mushroom Mardi Gras Cookoff, 2nd Place

Take a cue from the French. Mushrooms and chicken livers form a scintillating partnership.

8 large chicken livers

24 fresh large, white or brown mushrooms

6 tbsp. butter

8 tbsp. minced shallots or green onions with tops

7 large cloves garlic, minced or pressed

½ tsp. salt

½ tsp. pepper

½ tsp. Accent

½ tsp. Beau Monde

3 tbsp. hot water

1 tbsp. lemon juice

⅔ cup sherry wine

¼ cup diced bacon, drained, fried crisp, and crushed into bits

In a small saucepan, scald livers in hot water to cover, for about 3 minutes. Drain. Remove from pan, to cool.

With a small paring knife, remove stems from mushrooms. Finely chop stems. In a medium saucepan, melt butter. Sauté on medium-high: mushroom stems, shallots, garlic, salt, pepper, Accent, and Beau Monde for 3 minutes.

Cut up chicken livers, removing any membrane. Add to pan. Sauté 2 minutes longer. Add 3 tablespoons water and lemon juice. Continue cooking for 3 minutes. Cool. Pour liver-mushroom mixture into blender or food processor. Blend, adding sherry a little at a time to make a smooth paté. Place in medium bowl. Dip in bacon crumbs. Fill caps with paté. Arrange in broiler pan and chill till ready to serve. Broil about 8 minutes, 5 inches from flame. Serve at once. Serves 15-18.

Boca Mushrooms

Pete Kelley, Chef, Pete's Southside Cafe, San Louis Obispo, California

The Spanish word *boca* means "mouth." In South America, in a *boca* bar, before-dinner conversation takes place in a separate room, with participants standing around high tables, eating *tapas*, appetizers (as explained by Timothy's nephew, Frank Kelley, assistant manager).

2 lbs. fresh medium white
 mushrooms

½ cup green onion, chopped

4 cloves garlic, chopped

½ tsp. oregano, powdered

1 tsp. salt

1 tsp. pepper

1 cup red wine vinegar

4 cups water

1 can (6 oz.) diced pimientos

In a large pot, combine mushrooms, onion, garlic, oregano, salt, pepper, vinegar, and water. Simmer, covered, for 15 minutes or until mushrooms are tender. Cool, and add pimientos. Serves 12-15.

"There is something absolutely fascinating to me about being present at the exact moment when a mushroom is mushrooming."

John Cage, Avant-garde composer and founder of the
New York Mycological Society

Soups
& Sauces

Three Mushroom Soup with Roasted Garlic and Herbs

Brian G. Weselby, Regional Executive Chef,
California Café, Los Gatos, California

In March, 1993, President Bill Clinton and Vice President Al Gore came to Silicon Valley. President Clinton had requested that the dinner he and Al Gore shared with the business leaders of Silicon Valley be California Cuisine. They launched their gastronomic experiment with this dazzling soup. Brian and friends invite you to partake in the first course of a splendid dinner suitable for kings, presidents, and your family.

2 oz. olive oil

1 tsp. garlic, finely chopped

1 tsp. shallots, finely chopped

6 oz. Crimini (brown) mushrooms, sliced

6 oz. Oyster mushrooms, torn in small pieces

6 oz. Shiitake mushrooms, sliced

6 cups chicken stock

4 oz. grated potato

Salt, to taste

Pepper, to taste

1 tbsp. fresh thyme, finely chopped

¼ tsp. fresh rosemary, finely chopped

12 small grilled Shiitake mushrooms for garnish

18 whole cloves garlic, peeled and oven-roasted in olive oil

2 tbsp. chives, chopped

Heat olive oil in a large thick-bottomed saucepan. Add garlic and shallots. Sauté for 1 minute. Add sliced mushrooms and sauté until golden brown. Add chicken stock, potato, salt, and pepper. Bring to a boil and simmer for 30 minutes.

Blend half of the soup in a blender at slow speed. Add blended soup back into the pan. Add thyme and rosemary; cook 10 minutes longer. Garnish each serving with 2 grilled Shiitake mushrooms and 3 cloves garlic. Sprinkle with chopped chives. Serves 6.

Mushroom-Sherry Chicken Stock

Jim Gongwer, The First Light Cafe,
San Francisco, California

Home cooking is Jim and Margaret's specialty. Because they cook "from scratch" with natural, whole foods, their customers trust them and feel nurtured. Sometimes customers return for a second or third meal on the same day. With an uncanny sense for identifying the best in natural food, Jim captures the essence of the mushroom in this soup.

1½ tbsp. butter

1 medium onion, chopped

1 lb. fresh white mushrooms, diced irregularly

1½ quarts chicken stock

Juice of ½ lemon

½ cup sherry

¼ tsp. nutmeg

Pepper to taste

2 tbsp. fresh chives or parsley, chopped

In a large soup pot, melt butter and sauté onion until translucent, about 7 minutes, on medium-high heat. Add mushrooms and sauté, stirring for 3 more minutes. Pour in chicken stock, lemon juice, and sherry. Stir in nutmeg and pepper, to taste. Cover pot and simmer for 5 minutes. Divide soup into 4 to 6 bowls. Float chives or parsley on top of soup.

Serves 4-6.

Mushroom and Hazelnut Soup

Margaret Whelly, The First Light Cafe,
San Francisco, California

Mushrooms and nuts were important foods of ancient hunter-gatherer societies. Margaret pairs these two natural treasures in her simple, understated style.

4 tbsp. butter

2 medium yellow onions, chopped

1½ lb. fresh white mushrooms, chopped

1 quart vegetable stock

1 cup hazelnuts

In a large soup pot, melt butter. Sauté onions and mushrooms until the mushrooms begin to exude moisture. Add vegetable stock. Cover pot and bring to a boil; then let it simmer for 5 minutes. Cool. Pour soup into a food processor or blender. Process until smooth. Return to pot to re-heat for 10 minutes. On a cookie sheet, roast hazelnuts in oven on 450 degrees. Cool. Rub off skins. Grind hazelnuts in food processor or blender. Stir nuts into soup. Serve immediately.

Serves 10-12.

Mushroom Gazpacho

Courtesy of Monterey Mushrooms, Santa Cruz, California

Cool and refreshing, 89 calories per serving. Carl Fields at the main office, and Monterey Mushrooms' kitchen staff share this carefully-tested recipe with you and your family.

1 can (16 oz.) tomatoes, undrained

2 cups cucumber, peeled and chopped

$\frac{1}{2}$ cup green pepper, chopped

1 clove garlic, minced

2 tbsp. vegetable or olive oil

2 tbsp. red wine vinegar

$\frac{1}{2}$ tsp. salt

$\frac{1}{8}$ tsp. onion powder

2 drops bottled hot pepper sauce

$\frac{1}{2}$ lb. fresh white mushrooms,

1 can (12 oz.) tomato juice (1$\frac{1}{2}$ cups)

Snipped parsley

Put tomatoes, cucumber, green pepper, garlic, oil, vinegar, salt, onion powder, and pepper sauce into blender. Process until smooth. Coarsely chop half the mushrooms. Add to mixture in blender. Process until smooth. Pour into pitcher. Stir in tomato juice. Cover. Refrigerate 3 or 4 hours. Just before serving, coarsely chop remaining mushrooms. Stir into soup. Garnish servings with snipped parsley. Serves 6.

Three-Bean Mushroom Soup

Sandra L. Stewart and R. Timothy Haley

Whole cloves deliver a rich flavor to a colorful soup.

½ cup black beans

½ cup pink beans

½ cup white beans

8 cups water

1 whole onion, peeled and studded with cloves

3 cloves garlic, minced

2 tbsp. fresh chopped basil (or 1 tbsp. dried)

½ cup carrots, chopped

½ cup celery, chopped

½ cup red bell pepper, chopped

Hot pepper sauce, to taste

4 cups fresh large, white or brown mushrooms, chopped into large, irregular pieces

In a large soup pot, rinse beans and soak overnight or pre-cook for 1 hour. Pour off water. Add fresh water and onion-with-cloves. Cover and simmer for 3 to 5 hours. Slightly mash beans, onion, and cloves with pastry cutter or potato masher. Add garlic, basil, carrots, celery, bell pepper, and hot pepper sauce. Simmer for 45 minutes. Stir in mushrooms and simmer for 10 more minutes. Serve immediately. Place a small dollop of sour cream on each bowl of soup. Serves 6-8.

Mushroom Soup Alfredo

V. Sellers, Favorite Recipe Contest,
Morgan Hill's Mushroom Mardi Gras

Tomato paste and vermouth pack an extra punch to the nutty flavor of mushrooms.

3 tbsp. olive oil

3 tbsp. butter

2 cloves garlic, whole

1 medium onion, finely chopped

3 tbsp. tomato paste

1 lb. fresh white or brown mushrooms, sliced

4 cups hot chicken stock

2 tbsp. sweet Italian vermouth

2 tbsp. chopped parsley

4 egg yolks

In a large soup pot, heat oil and butter. Bruise garlic cloves by slightly crushing them against the pan with a large spoon. On medium heat, sauté for about 5 minutes. Remove garlic. Add onion and sauté for 5 more minutes. Raise heat under pan to medium-high. Add tomato paste and mushrooms, stirring to avoid burning. Add hot chicken stock and vermouth.

Boil for 2 minutes. Cool slightly. In a small bowl, whisk parsley with egg yolks; add a little hot soup. Whisk egg-parsley mixture into soup. Bring to a boil. Serve immediately. Serves 6-8.

Hungarian Cream Of Mushroom Soup

Dana Smith, Favorite Recipe Contest,
Morgan Hill's Mushroom Mardi Gras

Succulent mushrooms in an authentic, creamy soup.

½ lb. fresh white or brown mushrooms, thinly sliced

¼ cup margarine

1 tbsp. flour

1 tsp. paprika

2 tsp. chopped parsley

3 cups beef bouillon

1 tbsp. heavy cream

¾ cup dairy sour cream

1 egg yolk

In saucepan, sauté mushrooms in margarine for 6 minutes. Remove from heat. Blend in flour, paprika, and parsley. Add beef bouillon and cream. Cover and simmer 15 minutes. Remove from heat. In a medium bowl, blend sour cream and egg yolk.

Stir one cup of soup liquid into sour cream mixture; then, while stirring constantly, add sour cream mixture to remaining liquid in saucepan. Heat, but do not boil. Serves 5.

Mushroom Chicken Bouillon

Courtesy of Monterey Mushrooms, Santa Cruz, California

Light on the waistline, 18 calories per cup.

4 cups water

4 chicken bouillon cubes

½ tsp. onion powder

Dash white pepper

½ lb. fresh white mushrooms, sliced

2 tsp. chopped celery leaves

In large saucepan, heat water, bouillon, onion powder, and pepper until bouillon cubes dissolve. Stir in mushrooms and celery leaves. Heat to boiling. Reduce heat. Cover and simmer about 10 minutes or until mushrooms are tender. Serves 4-5.

Champignons a l'orange Sauce

Barry Wertz, 1st Place, Favorite Recipe Contest, Morgan Hill's Mushroom Mardi Gras

An award-winner. As a bonus, leftover broth, mushroom stems, and caps can star in other meals.

1 lb. fresh white mushrooms

⅔ cup medium dry sherry

⅛ tsp. celery seeds

1 tsp. onion powder

⅛ tsp. pepper, finely ground

Dash nutmeg

½ cup clarified butter*

⅔ cup frozen orange juice concentrate, thawed (do not dilute)

1 tsp. tarragon leaves

Salt, to taste

*To clarify butter, melt over low heat. Remove from heat and let butter stand a few minutes. Skim butter fat from the top and discard, leaving the clear yellow liquid.

Cut off mushroom stems flush with caps; set stems aside. Combine in a heavy skillet: mushroom caps, sherry, celery seed, onion powder, pepper and nutmeg. Simmer for 10 minutes over medium heat or until most of the moisture is rendered from the mushroom caps. Remove the mushrooms and retain the liquid.

In a separate saucepan, blend butter, orange concentrate, and tarragon leaves over medium heat. Add mushroom caps and simmer for 5 minutes, stirring frequently. Remove mushroom caps; set aside from sauce.

Serve with roast pheasant, duck, Cornish hens or chicken in an accompanying dish at the main course. Or, serve over a platter of poached fish. Serves 4-6.

Stems and Caps

Finely chop stems and mix with left over sherry and mushroom liquor. Can be used as gravy for main course or added to stock pot for another meal.

Mushrooms Barcelona Sauce

Courtesy of the Mushroom Council

A zesty variation on a Spanish theme. Serve with a side dish of fragrant rice. Listen to a lively *flamenco* while savoring your meal.

2 tbsp. butter or margarine

1 tbsp. vegetable oil

8 oz. fresh white mushrooms, quartered (about 3 cups)

½ cup chopped, toasted walnuts (optional)

2 tbsp. dry sherry

1 tbsp. lemon juice

1 tsp. grated orange or lemon peel

2 tbsp. chopped parsley

Salt, to taste

In medium skillet, combine butter and oil; heat to melt butter. Add mushrooms; sauté over medium-high heat until just tender, about 3 to 4 minutes. Add walnuts, sherry, lemon juice, and citrus peel; cook 1 minute longer. Sprinkle with parsley. Season with salt. Serve hot as an accompaniment to fish, chicken, or steak. Serves 4.

Basque Style Spanish Sauce

Pete Kelley, Pete's Southside Cafe,
San Luis Obispo, California

Transform an every-day fish or chicken dish with this saffron-laced sauce.

2 tbsp. olive oil

1 medium onion, chopped

1 bell pepper, chopped

½ cup celery, diced

3 cloves garlic, chopped

1 lb. fresh small white mushrooms

1 can (16 oz.) crushed tomatoes

1 can (6 oz.) diced pimientos

1 cup red wine

1 to 2 cups water

2 tsp. oregano

2 tsp. black pepper

2 tsp. salt

¼ tsp. saffron powder or saffron
  threads

1 can (6 oz.) sliced olives

1 tsp. capers

In a large saucepan, heat oil. Sauté onion, bell pepper, celery, garlic, and mushrooms until crisp-tender. Add tomatoes, pimientos, wine, water, oregano, pepper, salt, and saffron. Cover pan and simmer for half an hour. Add olives and capers. Serve immediately over seafood or poultry.

Serves 6-8.

...April starts to whisper to the trees;
I hoe and you plant the peas.
Canterbury Bells begin to ring,
The sparrows are stealing string.

Hollyhocks and Foxglove to the knee;
Now life's in a mojor key.
We've got mud between our toes,
This is how the garden grows....

Michael Franks, "How Our Garden Grows"
compact disc, *Passion Fruit*

Salads and Side Dishes

Shiitake Salad

Azumaya Inc. (Dried Mushrooms), San Francisco, California

Enjoy the earthy flavor of dried Shiitake in a zesty cumin sauce.

Salad
10 to 12 medium dried Shiitake
  mushrooms
½ red bell pepper, cut in julienne
  strips
½ red onion, sliced thinly

Dressing
½ cup olive oil
3 cloves garlic, mashed to a paste
2 tbsp. minced parsley
½ tsp. ground cumin
3 tbsp. lemon juice
Salt, to taste
Pepper, to taste

Soak mushrooms in warm water to cover until tender (about 30 minutes). Drain. Cut out and discard stems. Cut mushroom caps in halves or quarters. Add the red bell pepper strips. Add the sliced onions. Combine in a bowl with the mushrooms.

Whisk together oil, garlic, parsley, cumin, lemon juice, salt, and pepper, and fold gently into the mushroom salad. Marinate for at least 1 hour and serve at room temperature or chilled. Serves 4-6.

Shiitake Mushroom
Lentinus edodes

Stir-Fry Shiitake Mushrooms and Vegetables

Azumaya Inc. (Dried Mushrooms), San Francisco, California

A side dish to brilliantly complement fish, meat, or poultry; or a main dish, accompanied by rice.

½ cup (¾ oz.) dried Shiitake mushrooms

1 tbsp. cornstarch

1 tbsp. cool water

1 cup chicken broth, regular strength

1 tbsp. soy sauce

2 tbsp. peanut oil or salad oil

½ tsp. minced, fresh ginger

1 small clove garlic, minced

1 cup broccoli flowerets

1 cup carrots, thinly sliced

1 cup onions, thinly sliced

1 cup green or red bell pepper, thinly sliced

1 can (2½ oz.) water chestnuts, drained and sliced

Soak mushrooms in warm water to cover for thirty minutes. Drain. Remove and discard stems. Cut into bite-sized pieces.

In small bowl, blend cornstarch and water. Stir in broth and soy sauce and set aside.

In a wok or non-stick skillet, heat oil on high. Add ginger, garlic, broccoli, carrots, onions, bell pepper, and mushrooms. Stir-fry for 5 or 6 minutes.

Stir cornstarch mixture to blend; add to vegetables, along with water chestnuts. Cook, stirring, until sauce boils, thickens, and turns clear. Serves 4-6.

Pineapple-Mushroom Salad

Courtesy of Monterey Mushrooms, Santa Cruz, California

A scrumptious dinner salad. 97 calories per serving. (To reduce serving to 54 calories, omit almonds.)

1½ tbsp. cornstarch

1 tbsp. brown sugar

½ tsp. dry mustard

¼ tsp. ground ginger

1 can (8 oz.) unsweetened, crushed pineapple, undrained

⅓ cup catsup

1¼ cups water

1 lb. fresh white mushrooms, sliced

Lettuce leaves

½ cup toasted slivered almonds

Combine cornstarch, brown sugar, mustard, and ginger in medium-sized saucepan. Stir in pineapple, catsup, and water. Cook and stir over medium heat until boiling and clear. Chill, covered, several hours or overnight. (Dressing will thicken.)

About 1 hour before serving, combine mushrooms and pineapple mixture. Refrigerate. To serve, divide among 8 lettuce-lined salad plates. Top each with 1 tablespoon almonds. Serves 8.

Creamy Mushroom Salad

Courtesy of Monterey Mushrooms, Santa Cruz, California

Low in calories, high in flavor. 6 servings: 86 calories per serving; 8 servings: 65 calories per serving.

$2/3$ cup dairy sour cream

2 tbsp. green onions with tops, finely chopped

$1/4$ tsp. salt

$1/8$ tsp. dill weed, crushed

Dash white pepper

$1/4$ cup skim milk

1 lb. fresh white mushrooms, sliced

2 tbsp. lemon juice

$3/4$ lb. Bibb lettuce or salad greens

Capers (optional)

Combine sour ceam, onions, salt, dill weed, and pepper. Stir in milk until well blended. Cover and chill at least 2 hours. Divide lettuce among 6 to 8 chilled salad plates. Toss mushrooms with lemon juice. Place on lettuce. Top with chilled sour cream dressing. Garnish with capers, if desired. Serves 6-8.

Mushroom-Orange Toss

Courtesy of Monterey Mushrooms, Santa Cruz, California

An unusual taste combination. 59 calories per serving.

5 cups torn lettuce

2 seedless oranges, peeled, sliced into eighths, and quartered

½ lb. fresh white mushrooms, thickly sliced

½ cup thinly-sliced red onion rings, separated

½ cup low-calorie French-style dressing

Lettuce leaves

Toss lettuce, orange pieces, mushrooms, and onion rings with dressing until well coated. Serve on lettuce leaves. Serves 8.

Mushroom-stuffed Tomatoes

Courtesy of Monterey Mushrooms, Santa Cruz, California

A cool, cool luncheon salad. 155 calories per serving.

½ cup dairy sour cream

2 hard-cooked eggs, finely chopped

½ tsp. chopped chives

½ tsp. seasoned salt

¼ tsp. celery salt

Dash garlic powder

4 large tomatoes

½ lb. fresh white mushrooms, coarsely chopped

Lettuce leaves

Paprika

In a medium bowl, combine sour cream, eggs, chives, seasoned salt, celery salt, and garlic. Chill. On a serving plate garnished with lettuce leaves, turn each tomato, stem side down. Cut to, but not through base into 6 wedges. Spread wedges apart slightly. Salt lightly. Just before serving, toss sour cream mixture with mushrooms. Divide among prepared tomatoes. Garnish with paprika. Serves 4.

B.L.T. Salad

Courtesy of Monterey Mushrooms, Santa Cruz, California

A new twist to an old favorite. Serve with crackers or melba toast. 172 calories per serving.

4 firm large tomatoes

Lettuce leaves

1 lb. fresh white mushrooms, sliced

8 strips crisp fried bacon, crumbled

4 green onions with tops, thinly sliced

3 tbsp. vegetable oil

1 tbsp. red wine vinegar

1½ tsp. salt

⅛ tsp. black pepper

Cut 18 center slices from tomatoes. Lightly salt. Arrange in 6 lettuce-lined salad bowls. Coarsely chop tomato ends in a medium bowl; toss with mushrooms, bacon, onions, oil, vinegar, salt, and pepper. Spoon over tomato slices. Serves 6.

Tuna Mushroom Slaw

Courtesy of Monterey Mushrooms, Santa Cruz, California

For even fewer calories, substitute plain, lowfat yogurt for half the sour cream. 184 calories per serving.

⅔ cup dairy sour cream

1 tbsp. finely-chopped onion

1½ tsp. salt

⅛ tsp. dill weed

Dash pepper

1 can (6½ oz.) chunk light water-pack tuna, drained and flaked

1 hard-cooked egg, finely chopped

½ lb. fresh white mushrooms, sliced

1½ cups shredded cabbage

1 tbsp. pimiento, finely-chopped

Lettuce leaves

Paprika

4 green pepper rings

Combine sour cream, onion, salt, dill weed, and pepper. Chill. Just before serving, toss in tuna, egg, mushrooms, cabbage, and pimiento. Serve on lettuce leaves. Garnish with paprika and green pepper rings. Serves 4.

Curried Chicken Salad

Courtesy of Monterey Mushrooms, Santa Cruz, California

Extra delicious with fresh mushrooms and grapes. 212 calories per serving.

⅔ cup dairy sour cream

¼ to ½ tsp. curry powder

⅛ tsp. salt

⅛ tsp. ground ginger

Dash garlic powder

½ lb. fresh white mushrooms, sliced

1½ cups cooked chicken, diced

½ cup seedless green grapes, halved

2 firm medium tomatoes, sliced into
  6 slices each

Lettuce leaves

Paprika

Parsley

Combine sour cream, curry powder, salt, ginger, and garlic powder. Chill, covered, for several hours. Just before serving, toss with mushrooms, chicken, and grapes.

Lightly salt tomato slices. For each serving, arrange 3 tomato slices on lettuce leaves. Top with mushroom mixture. Garnish with paprika and parsley. Serves 4.

Garden-Fresh Mushroom Salad with Next-to-Nothing Dressing

Courtesy of Monterey Mushrooms, Santa Cruz, California

Extra light and delicious. Without dressing, 18 calories per serving. Dressing contains 3½ calories per tablespoon.

6 cups torn salad lettuce

½ lb. fresh small white mushrooms, sliced

½ cup sliced cucumber

⅓ cup sliced red radishes

2 green onions, with tops, sliced

Toss lettuce, mushrooms, cucumber, radishes, and green onions in salad bowl. Divide among 8 salad plates. Add Next-to-Nothing Dressing just before serving. Serves 8.

Next-to-Nothing Dressing

1 can (12 oz.) tomato juice (1½ cups)

⅓ cup chopped celery

¼ cup chopped onion

2 tbsp. chopped green bell pepper

2 tsp. lemon juice

1 tsp. sugar

1 tsp. garlic salt

¼ tsp. Worcestershire sauce

Next-To-Nothing Dressing

Place all ingredients in blender. Process until smooth. Cover and refrigerate at least 4 hours to blend flavors. Dressing may be stored up to 2 weeks. Makes 2 cups.

Peruvian Potato-Mushroom Salad

Sandra L. Stewart and R. Timothy Haley

Who says mushrooms and Latin foods don't mix! Mushrooms go spicy in this South American salad.

½ lb. fresh small white mushrooms, whole

1½ lb. small, new potatoes, boiled in jackets

½ lb. cheddar cheese, grated

4 yolks of hard boiled eggs

3 mashed chilies or 1 tsp. chili powder

1 tsp. salt

¼ tsp. pepper

¼ cup olive oil

1 cup evaporated milk

½ tsp. lemon juice

½ cup onion, minced

Lettuce and olives for garnish

In a saucepan, boil mushrooms for 2 or 3 minutes. Drain. Place the mushrooms on a serving platter. Cool and peel the boiled potatoes and mix them with the mushrooms.

In a medium bowl, mash the cheese with the egg yolks. Add the mashed chilies or chili powder, salt, and pepper, and beat well with a wooden spoon. Add the olive oil, little by little. Add the milk and lemon juice. Add the minced onion and adjust the seasonings to taste.

Cover the potatoes and mushrooms with sauce, and garnish the platter with lettuce and olives. Serve cold. Serves 6-8.

Mushroom-Potato Salad with Caraway Dressing

Sandra L. Stewart and R. Timothy Haley

An American potluck staple, transfigured by mushrooms and a gourmet dressing.

Salad

Six large red potatoes, unpeeled

1½ cups fresh small white mushrooms, finely chopped (reserve 4 or 5 mushrooms for garnish)

4 hard boiled eggs (finely chop 3 eggs; reserve 1 egg for garnish)

½ cup onion, diced

½ cup celery, diced

½ cup red bell pepper, diced

1 tsp. celery seed

1 tsp. garlic powder

2 tsp. white pepper

Salt, to taste

Caraway Dressing

1 egg

2 tbsp. wine vinegar or lemon juice

½ tsp. dry mustard

⅔ cup olive oil

1 tbsp. onion, grated

1 tbsp. caraway seeds

1 tsp. sugar

Salad

In a 5-quart pan, gently boil the potatoes, covered, until tender. Cool. Dice the potatoes, skins on, and combine them in a large bowl with mushrooms, chopped eggs, onion, celery, bell pepper, celery seed, garlic powder, white pepper, and salt.

Stir in the caraway dressing. Mix thoroughly.

Garnish with egg slices topped by mushroom slices. Chill for 1 hour. Serves 6-8.

Caraway Dressing

Put the egg, vinegar or lemon juice, and mustard in a blender. Add 2 tablespoons oil very slowly, on low speed. Pour in remaining oil in a stream. Blend. Pour dressing into a small bowl. Add onion, caraway seeds, and sugar. Stir gently, to mix.

Marinated Relish Salad

Linda Tarvin, Favorite Recipe Contest,
Morgan Hill's Mushroom Mardi Gras

A sweet-and-sour medley of mushrooms and fresh vegetables.

2 lb. fresh small white mushrooms, whole

2 cups bean sprouts

2 cups raw cauliflower, cut in small flowerets

1 medium cucumber, peeled and thinly sliced

1 green pepper, cut into thin strips

⅔ cup green onion, chopped

1⅔ cups vinegar

¼ cup honey

⅔ cup salad or olive oil

2 cloves garlic, minced

½ tsp. salt

20 cherry tomatoes, halved

Combine mushrooms, sprouts, cauliflower, cucumber, green pepper, and onion. In a sealed jar, combine vinegar, honey, oil, garlic, and salt. Shake well. Pour over vegetables; toss lightly. Cover and chill several hours or overnight.

Before serving, add tomatoes; toss lightly. Serves 12-15.

Mario's Marinated Mushroom Salad

Courtesy of Chef Mario Barbaglia, Bon Apetít Square,
Morgan Hill's Mushroom Mardi Gras

Just one of the heavenly taste treats waiting for you at the Mardi Gras.

2½ lb. fresh large mushrooms, sliced to ⅛ inch thickness

1½ cups fresh parsley, finely chopped

2 cups diced celery

6 cloves of fresh garlic, finely chopped

1 cup olive oil

¼ cup red wine vinegar

½ cup lemon juice

1 tbsp. Italian seasoning

1½ tbsp. coarse black pepper

Salt, to taste

Put mushrooms in a bowl along with the parsley, celery, and garlic. Mix together oil, vinegar, lemon juice, and seasonings. Pour over the vegetables and blend well. Marinate 2 to 3 hours before serving. Serves 4-6.

Mushroom-Vegetable Greens with Lemon Caper Dressing

Sandra L. Stewart and R. Timothy Haley

A fresh, tangy dressing over your favorite "greens" and carrots.

2 tbsp. olive oil

3 cloves garlic, minced

1 small onion, diced

2 large carrots, peeled and cut lengthwise into thin, 3-inch strips

½ lb. fresh small white mushrooms, halved

½ cup fresh lemon juice, strained

2 tbsp. capers, drained

1 bunch Swiss chard, or 2 bunches spinach, torn into large pieces

In a large wok or skillet, heat oil on medium-high. Add garlic, onion, carrots, and mushrooms. Stir-fry until crisp-tender. Stir in lemon juice, capers, and greens. Stir-fry for 5 more minutes. Serve immediately. Serves 6.

Vegetable Stir-Fry

Courtesy of Monterey Mushrooms, Santa Cruz, California

Tender, crisp vegetables in a lightly seasoned sauce. 99 calories per serving.

1 chicken bouillon cube

¼ cup warm water

1 clove garlic, minced

3 tbsp. vegetable oil

¼ tsp. salt

½ lb. fresh large white mushrooms, thickly sliced

1 cup thinly-sliced yellow summer squash

½ cup bias-cut celery

¼ cup green pepper strips

¼ cup carrots, thinly-sliced

2 small tomatoes, cut in wedges

1 to 1½ tbsp. cornstarch

1 tbsp. soy sauce

Soften bouillon cube in water. Set aside. In large skillet or wok, cook garlic in oil and salt over low heat, until browned. Increase heat to high. Add mushrooms, squash, celery, green pepper, and carrots. Cook and stir 3 minutes. Reduce heat to medium. Add bouillon-water and tomatoes. Cover. Cook 3 minutes.

Combine cornstarch and soy sauce. Stir into vegetables. Cook, uncovered, over high heat until sauce thickens and bubbles, about 1 minute. Serves 6.

Mushroom Stuffing

Courtesy of Monterey Mushrooms, Santa Cruz, California

A nice, moist vegetable stuffing to serve with poultry or meat. Makes enough for a 5 to 6 pound capon. 74 calories per serving.

⅓ cup water

1 chicken bouillon cube

1 tsp. seasoned salt

1 tsp. rubbed sage

Dash pepper

1 tbsp. diet imitation margarine

1¼ cups diced celery

¾ cup diced carrots

⅔ cup chopped onion

1 lb. fresh white mushrooms, coarsely chopped

4 slices slightly dry wheat bread, cubed

In 3-quart saucepan, heat together water, bouillon cube, salt, sage, pepper, and margarine until bouillon cube is dissolved. Add celery, carrots, and onion. Heat to boiling. Reduce heat. Cover. Simmer 5 minutes. Stir in mushrooms. Cover and simmer 5 minutes longer, stirrng occasionally. Remove from heat. Add bread. Mix until thoroughly moistened. Turn into shallow 1½-quart baking dish. Bake at 350 degrees for 30 minutes or until top is dry. Serves 8.

Mushroom-Vegetable Kabobs

Courtesy of Monterey Mushrooms, Santa Cruz, California

A delightfully seasoned dish. 63 calories per serving.

1 lb. large fresh white mushrooms

1 large green pepper, cut into $1\frac{1}{4}$ x $\frac{1}{2}$-inch strips

2 to 3 small zucchini, cut into $\frac{1}{4}$-inch slices

$\frac{1}{3}$ cup diet imitation margarine, melted

$\frac{1}{2}$ tsp. seasoned salt

$\frac{1}{4}$ tsp. garlic powder

8 cherry tomatoes

Thread mushrooms, green pepper, and zucchini alternately onto skewers. Lay skewers on a large cookie sheet. Combine margarine, salt, and garlic powder. Lightly brush on vegetables. Broil about 4 minutes, 3 inches from flame. Turn. Place tomatoes on ends of skewers. Brush with remaining margarine mixture. Continue to broil to desired doneness. Serves 8.

Linguini with Mushrooms

Courtesy of Monterey Mushrooms, Santa Cruz, California

An inviting flavor combination. Use larger servings for a meatless main dish.

4 oz. linguini, broken in thirds (2 cups cooked)

1 clove garlic, minced

1 cup thinly-sliced carrots

2 tbsp. butter or margarine

1 lb. fresh medium white mushrooms, sliced

1 tsp all-purpose flour

½ tsp. onion salt

¼ tsp. Italian herb seasoning

Dash pepper

3 tbsp. grated Parmesan cheese

Snipped parsley

Cook linguini according to package directions. Drain. Meanwhile, sauté garlic and carrots in butter over high heat about 3 minutes. Add mushrooms. Sauté about 3 minutes more or just until liquid begins to form. In a small bowl, combine flour, onion salt, Italian seasoning, and pepper. Sprinkle over mushrooms. Continue to heat and stir until part of liquid has evaporated and mushrooms are coated with a thin sauce. Add linguini. Sprinkle with Parmesan. Toss. Sprinkle with snipped parsley. Serve immediately. Serves 6.

Mushrooms with Grapes

Jayne Chick, Favorite Recipe Contest Finalist,
Morgan Hill's Mushroom Mardi Gras

Right out of the mushroom farms and vineyards of central California's coast!

20 coriander seeds

⅔ cup olive oil

8 oz. fresh small white mushrooms
 (cut in half)

30 seedless grapes (cut in half)

Juice of 1 orange

½ bay leaf

1 small clove garlic (run through
 press)

Pinch of salt

1 tsp. brown sugar

1 squeeze of lemon juice

Place coriander seeds in large pan and crush with back of wooden spoon. Add oil and cook over medium heat for 2 minutes. Add mushrooms; cook 2 minutes more. Add grapes, orange juice, bay leaf, garlic, salt, sugar, and lemon juice, and simmer for 5 minutes. With slotted spoon remove grapes and mushrooms to a heated serving dish. Continue cooking, uncovered, to reduce sauce to a concentrated flavor. Pour over mushrooms. Serve hot over rice. Serves 4.

Mushrooms a la Barberi

Courtesy of Morgan Hill's Mushroom Mardi Gras
Recipe and Cookoff Committee Member, John Barberi

Whip up this Sauterne and tomato-mushroom sauce for an intimate, romantic dinner. Goes well with any baked, grilled, or BBQ meat or poultry. Don't forget the French bread.

½ lb. fresh small white mushrooms

2 tsp. olive oil or butter

1 clove garlic, pressed

¼ cup Sauterne wine

1 heaping tbsp. tomato paste

Salt, to taste

Pepper, to taste

⅔ cup cool water

1 tsp. cornstarch

1 tsp. parsley, minced

*Blanch mushrooms in boiling water for 1 minute. Drain and cool. Then quarter or thickly slice mushrooms.

In a heavy skillet, heat oil on high. Add mushrooms and sauté until light brown. Add garlic and stir well. Stir in wine, tomato paste, salt, and pepper. Simmer for 3 minutes. In a cup mix water and cornstarch until smooth; add to mushroom mixture and cook, stirring until glossy. Sprinkle with parsley and serve immediately.
Serves 2.

*To blanch, plunge mushrooms in boiling water. Remove and place in cold water to stop the cooking process.

English mushroom hunters sometimes call Oyster mushrooms the shellfish of the wood.

Since the eating of meat is banned by the Buddhist religion, Shiitakes play a major role in Zen monastery cooking.

"Shiitakes. . . carry their smoky flavor through the strongest of seasonings."

Doug Peacock, "The Mushroom Chronicles," *Outside*

Main Dishes

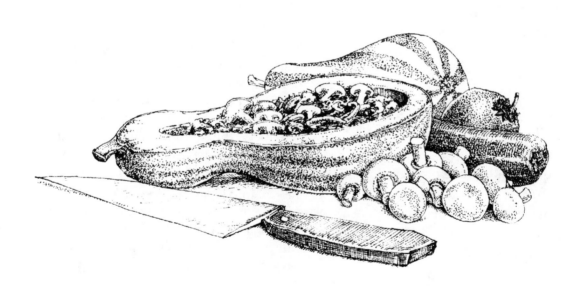

Louisiana Grits Cakes with Mushroom and Prosciutto Gravy

Sandra L. Stewart and R. Timothy Haley

Southern soul food with a contemporary touch. The grits cakes are a version of Sandra's grandma's "fried mush."

Grits Cakes

4 cups chicken broth

¼ cup butter

2½ cups regular, yellow grits

1 cup whipping cream

Salt, to taste

White pepper, to taste

Cornmeal

Vegetable or canola oil

Mushroom and Prosciutto Gravy

¼ cup butter

⅔ cup flour

1 quart cold, strong chicken stock, low salt

4 or 5 drops hot pepper sauce

2 cups fresh medium, white or brown mushrooms, thinly sliced

3 oz. Prosciutto, diced

Grits Cakes

In a large saucepan, bring chicken broth and butter to boil. Stir in grits. Continue boiling and reduce heat, stirring to keep grits from scorching; cook about 30 minutes, stirring often (add additional stock if grits get too thick). Add cream and cook another 20 minutes, stirring often. Season with salt and white pepper to taste.

Line a large shallow pan or two small, shallow pans with waxed paper. After grits have cooled slightly and are a thick mass, pour into lined pan and spread out about 1 inch thick. Chill until firm. Using biscuit and cookie cutters, cut chilled grits into desired shapes and dust with cornmeal.

Pour oil into heavy skillet to cover bottom to depth of ⅛ inch; heat over medium-high flame. Pan-fry grits cakes on both sides until crispy. Pour Mushroom and Prosciutto gravy over grits cakes before serving. Serves 6-8.

Mushroom and Prosciutto Gravy

In a heavy skillet, melt butter on low heat. Add flour. Continue to cook over very low heat, 2 to 5 minutes, stirring constantly until flour has a nutty aroma. Slowly add cold chicken stock, stirring constantly with whisk. Increase heat to high and continue stirring until gravy comes to a boil. Whisk vigorously to get out the lumps. Add pepper sauce, mushrooms, and prosciutto. Simmer gravy 10 to 15 minutes. Serve over pan-fried grits cakes. Serves 6-8.

Mushroom Turkey Piquant

Courtesy of Monterey Mushrooms, Santa Cruz, California

A great way to enjoy left-over turkey.

2 tbsp. butter or margarine

2 tbsp. vegetable oil

1 lb. fresh white mushrooms, sliced

4 slices turkey breast (about 3 oz. each) pounded to ⅛-inch thickness

Flour

¼ cup dry sherry

⅔ cups chicken broth

½ cup lemon juice

¼ cup water

¼ cup capers, drained

Salt, to taste

Pepper, to taste

Watercress

1 lemon

In large skillet, heat 1 tablespoon each butter and oil to sizzling. Add mushrooms; sauté over medium heat until tender but still firm. Remove to warm platter and set aside. Dust turkey slices generously with flour. Sauté in remaining butter and oil, 3 to 5 minutes, turning once when edges of turkey become opaque. Remove turkey to platter with mushrooms. Stir an additional teaspoon of flour into skillet. Stir in sherry, then broth, lemon juice, and water. Simmer 5 minutes. Stir in mushrooms, turkey, and capers. Season with salt and pepper. Simmer to heat through. Garnish each serving with watercress and lemon slices. Serves 4.

Mushrooms with Alabama Sauce and Grits

Sandra L. Stewart and R. Timothy Haley

Embrace your family with rich American tradition while introducing the succulence of mushrooms. A southern comfort food that deserves to be added to your vegetarian menu. Serve with buttermilk biscuits and honey, cole slaw, and chilled apple cider.

3 tbsp. butter

5 cups fresh white or brown mushrooms, thinly sliced

$\frac{1}{4}$ cup onion, finely chopped

$\frac{1}{3}$ cup dry white wine

water

3 tbsp. flour

1 tbsp. Worcestershire sauce

Salt, to taste

Pepper, to taste

$\frac{1}{8}$ tsp. nutmeg

1 recipe basic grits

Quick Grits

4 cups water

1 tsp. salt

1 cup regular grits

In a large, heavy skillet, heat 1 tablespoon butter. Add mushrooms and onion and cook over medium heat, covered, until mushrooms exude broth. Separate mushrooms from broth and set aside. In a saucepan, combine broth with wine and water to make $1\frac{1}{2}$ cups.

In skillet, on low heat, melt remaining 2 tablespoons butter. Add flour and cook over medium-low heat, stirring constantly until butter is absorbed and mixture turns light brown. Remove skillet from heat. Do not boil. Gradually whisk in mushroom liquid and Worcestershire sauce, stirring vigorously. When gravy is thick and smooth, add reserved mushrooms. Season with salt, pepper, and nutmeg. Lower heat, cover, and simmer 3 to 4 minutes. Serve immediately over quick grits. Serves 4.

Quick Grits
In a saucepan, combine 4 cups water and 1 teaspoon salt. Bring to a boil. Stir in grits. Reduce heat to lowest setting and cook, covered, 15 to 20 minutes, stirring occasionally. Serves 4.

Ginger Mushroom Stir-Fry
Courtesy of Monterey Mushrooms, Santa Cruz, California

Features fresh mushrooms, chicken, and asparagus in a one-dish, Chinese meal. Serve hot, over rice.

3 tbsp. lemon juice

3 tbsp. soy sauce

1 tbsp. grated, fresh ginger

2 cloves garlic, pressed

2 skinned, boned, chicken breast halves, cut into strips, about ½-inch thick

2 tsp. cornstarch

⅓ cup chicken broth or bouillon

2 tbsp. vegetable oil

8 oz. fresh white mushrooms, quartered

1½ cups fresh asparagus slices, about 1½ inches long

3 green onions, sliced diagonally into 1-inch pieces

Toasted sesame seeds

1 lemon

8 sprigs cilantro

In a bowl, combine lemon juice, soy sauce, ginger, and garlic. Add chicken, tossing to coat; set aside. In measuring cup, dissolve cornstarch in broth; set aside.

In wok or skillet, heat oil to sizzling. Add mushrooms and drained chicken. (Reserve liquid.) Toss over high heat until chicken loses its pink color. Add asparagus and onions. Continue to toss over high heat until chicken is cooked and vegetables are crisp-tender. Stir in liquid drained from chicken and cornstarch-broth mixture to thicken. Sprinkle with sesame seeds. Garnish with lemon slices and cilantro. Serves 4.

Louisiana Grits Soufflé with Mushroom Creole Sauce

Sandra L. Stewart and R. Timothy Haley

Another vegetarian recipe from our country kitchen. This one is elegant enough for a formal dinner, southern style.

Louisiana Grits Soufflé

½ cup grits

2½ cups boiling water

1 tsp. salt

3 eggs, separated*

2 tbsp. butter or margarine

⅛ tsp. cream of tartar

Mushroom Creole Sauce

⅓ cup vegetable or canola oil

4 tbsp. flour

1 large onion, chopped

1 red bell pepper, chopped

2 cloves garlic, crushed

1 can (6 oz.) tomato paste

2¼ cups low salt chicken broth

1 lb. fresh medium, white or brown
  mushrooms, thinly sliced

Salt, to taste

Pepper, to taste

*Tip: a quick, easy way to separate eggs—crack egg gently against the rim of a small mixing bowl. Hold half of broken egg in each hand over bowl. Carefully pour yolk from one half shell to the other half shell and back again, repeatedly, until all egg white has dripped into the bowl. Place separated egg yolk in a separate bowl.

In a saucepan, slowly stir grits into boiling water. Add salt, cover, and cook until grits are done (about 3 minutes for quick grits), stirring once or twice while cooking. Remove from heat and beat in egg yolks and butter. Simmer for 3 minutes. Beat egg whites until foamy. Add cream of tartar and continue to beat until stiff peaks form. Fold into grits. Turn into well-greased, 1½ quart soufflé or deep baking dish. Bake at 400 degrees for 30 minutes or until puffed and brown. Serve immediately with Mushroom Creole Sauce.

Serves 4-6.

Mushroom Creole Sauce

In a large skillet or Dutch oven, heat oil. Stir in flour and cook over low heat, stirring until golden brown. Add onion, red pepper, and garlic. Cook, stirring, until onion is soft. Add tomato paste and chicken broth. Bring to a boil, stirring well. Reduce heat; simmer, uncovered, stirring occasionally. Add mushrooms, salt, and pepper to taste. Heat thoroughly for 10 minutes, simmering. Serve with Grits Soufflé. Serves 4-6.

Summer Spaghetti with Fresh Tomato and Mushroom Sauce

Courtesy of Monterey Mushrooms, Santa Cruz, California

This vegetarian sauce and spaghetti may also be served chilled.

3 cups finely chopped ripe tomatoes

⅔ cup chopped bell pepper

¼ cup chopped green onions

¼ cup chopped parsley

2 cloves garlic, pressed

1 tbsp. red wine vinegar

Salt, to taste

Hot pepper sauce, to taste

8 oz. fresh white or brown mushrooms, sliced

12 oz. spaghetti, cooked and drained

In mixing bowl, combine tomatoes, bell pepper, onions, parsley, garlic, vinegar, salt, and hot pepper sauce. Add mushrooms, tossing to mix well. Cook spaghetti in boiling, salted water until just tender. Drain. Serve sauce at room temperature over warm spaghetti. Serves 6.

Mushroom Enchiladas with Tomatillo Sauce

Pete's Southside Café, San Luis Obispo, California

Chef and restaurant owner, Pete Kelly, has created a unique Caribbean-Latin cuisine. Mushrooms are a central ingredient in this popular dish. Serve with beans and rice.

Tomatillo Sauce

1 can (16 oz.) pureed tomatillos

5 fresh jalapeños, finely chopped

1 green bell pepper, finely chopped

3 cloves garlic, finely chopped

1 tsp. ground cumin

½ tsp. ground cloves

½ cup onion, finely chopped

Juice of 2 fresh lemons

1 tsp. salt

1 cup water

½ cup milk

½ cup flour

Enchiladas

½ lb. margarine

2 cups white or brown mushrooms, chopped

Olive oil

12 corn tortillas

1 lb. jack cheese, grated

Tomatillo Sauce

In a large saucepan, combine tomatillos, jalapeños, bell pepper, garlic, cumin, cloves, onion, lemon juice, salt, and water. Simmer for ½ hour, covered. In a jar or bowl, mix milk and flour together until there are no lumps, and whisk the mixture into the tomatillo sauce.

Enchiladas

In large skillet, melt margarine and sauté mushrooms for 5 minutes. Set mushrooms and butter-broth aside. Add 2 tablespoons olive oil to skillet. Lightly fry tortillas in medium-hot oil until soft. In a large baking pan, or casserole, fill tortillas with mushrooms and jack cheese and a small amount of the sauce. Fold tortillas over and cover with tomatillo sauce and jack cheese. Bake in a pre-heated, 350-degree oven for 10 minutes, or until cheese is melted.
Serves 12.

Chicken Sausage and Oyster Mushroom pasta with Asparagus

Sandra L. Stewart and R. Timothy Haley

A one-dish meal of exotic California cuisine.

2 large (1 lb.) spicy chicken sausages, cut in 1-inch pieces

3 tbsp. olive oil

½ cup onion, diced

2 cloves garlic, minced

½ lb. fresh asparagus tips

½ cup Roma tomatoes, quartered

1 tbsp. capers

Juice of 1 lemon

4 large fresh Oyster mushrooms, torn in bite-sized pieces

8 cups water

½ lb. fresh fettucine pasta

1 cup fresh, grated Parmesan cheese

In a large skillet, sauté sausage until light brown and tender. Do not overcook. Remove from skillet and set aside. Scrape out skillet. Add olive oil; heat on medium. Sauté onion, garlic, and asparagus tips until asparagus is crisp-tender. Add tomatoes, capers, lemon juice, and mushrooms. Add sausage pieces. Simmer, covered, for 5 minutes. In a medium-sized pot, boil water with remaining tablespoon olive oil. Add fettucine and boil for 8 to 10 minutes, or until *al dente*. Divide pasta onto 4 serving plates. Pour sausage-mushroom mixture over noodles. Serve immediately with Parmesan cheese and French bread. Serves 4.

Pork Rolls with Mushroom-Shallot Sauce

Sandra L. Stewart and R. Timothy Haley

Tender cheese-stuffed pork with a superb sauce. Serve with fresh sautéed vegetables and whole wheat rolls.

Pork Rolls

1 lb. fresh pork butt cut into 4 scallops, pounded thinly

4 tbsp. grated, imported, Asagio cheese

1 cup dry, white wine

2 tbsp. olive oil

Mushroom Shallot Sauce

2 tbsp. unsalted butter

4 oz. fresh white or brown mushrooms, finely chopped

2 tbsp. shallots, finely chopped

2 tsp. fresh lemon juice

Freshly ground pepper, to taste

4-6 sprigs cilantro

Parmesan cheese

Pork Rolls

Sprinkle 1 tablespoon cheese on each of the 4 pork scallops. Roll each scallop into a roll. In a large skillet, heat olive oil to medium-high. Add pork rolls and brown on all sides, turning often, for 10 minutes. Stir in wine and simmer pork rolls on low heat, covered, for 20 minutes.

Mushroom-Shallot Sauce

In a saucepan, melt butter and sauté mushrooms and shallots for 5 minutes. Add lemon juice and cook for 2 more minutes. Add pepper, stirring. Arrange a pork roll on each of 4 plates. Pour a serving of mushroom-shallot sauce over each roll. Garnish each plate with cilantro. Serve with Parmesan cheese. Serves 4.

BBQ Pizza

Duane Murray, Mushroom's Grille and Bar Restaurant,
Morgan Hill, California

Make this smoky, vegetarian, gourmet treat in your own back yard.

Pizza

2 tbsp. butter

2 tbsp. olive oil

2 tbsp. sherry

½ cup fresh white or brown
   mushrooms, sliced thinly

One 12-inch pre-cooked pizza shell

⅓ cup pizza sauce

1 cup grated mozzarella cheese

1 tsp. dried basil leaves

Pizza Sauce

¼ cup olive oil

½ cup onion, finely chopped

1½ tsp. garlic powder

1 can (15 oz.) tomato sauce

1 can (6 oz.) tomato paste

1 tbsp. basil, crushed

2 tsp. oregano

½ tsp. salt

½ tsp. black pepper

¼ tsp. cayenne pepper

1 tsp. lemon juice

2 tbsp. honey

¼ cup plus 2 tbsp. red wine

2 tsp. corn syrup

½ tsp. molasses

½ tsp. vinegar

Pizza

In a small saucepan, melt butter over medium heat. Add 1 tablespoon olive oil, sherry, and mushrooms. Sauté for 5 minutes. Set aside.

Coat both sides of pre-cooked pizza shell with remaining tablespoon olive oil. Spread sauce evenly over top of shell. Spread cheese over sauce. Sprinkle pre-cooked mushrooms on cheese. Sprinkle basil on pizza. Place pizza on round pan or flat cookie sheet. Bake over medium coals in covered BBQ kettle for approximately 15 minutes, or until cheese is melted. Serves 2-4.

Pizza Sauce

In medium saucepan, heat oil. Sauté onion until tender. Add garlic, tomato sauce, tomato paste, basil, oregano, salt, and black and cayenne peppers. Stir in lemon juice, honey, red wine, corn syrup, molasses, and vinegar. Simmer gently, covered, for 15 to 20 minutes. Makes enough sauce for three 12-inch pizzas.

San Joaquin Valley Chuck and Potatoes with Mushroom-Onion Gravy

Sandra L. Stewart and R. Timothy Haley

This recipe is adapted and written in honor of Barbra and Howard "Nick" Nicholson.

Mashed potatos

5 large red potatoes, boiled with skins on

3 tbsp. butter or margarine

1 tsp. salt

1 cup hot milk

Chuck and Gravy

1½ lb. fresh ground chuck

Seasoning salt, to taste (preferably Lawry's)

Pepper, to taste

1 tbsp. salad or canola oil

4 tbsp. butter or margarine

1 medium onion, chopped

1 lb. fresh white or brown mushrooms, thinly sliced

2 tbsp. Worcestershire sauce

2 tbsp. flour

sour cream

Horseradish

Spicy mustard

Pepper, to taste

Mashed Potatoes

In a mixing bowl, mash potatoes with an electric mixer until smooth, except for bits of skin. Add butter, salt, and milk. Beat with fork or heavy whisk until potatoes are creamy. Keep mashed potatoes warm by placing the bowl in a larger bowl of hot water and covering.

Chuck and Gravy

Form beef into 4 rectangular chuck patties, about 2 inches thick. Add seasoning salt and pepper. Pre-heat oil in a large, heavy skillet, or on a grill, and fry patties for 8 minutes on each side, over medium-high heat, uncovered (cooking time may vary. For medium-rare, fry for 7 minutes on each side), until both sides are a rich, crusty brown and the inside is pink. Do not overcook. Remove chuck to drain on a warm platter covered with a paper towel. Pour all oil from skillet, leaving bits of meat in pan.

Heat 2 tablespoons butter in the skillet. Sauté onion and mushrooms, stirring often, over medium-high heat for 8 minutes. Pour mushrooms, onion, and butter-broth into a saucepan and set aside. In a large measuring cup, separate mushroom-butter broth from mushrooms and add Worcestershire sauce to make 1 cup.

Melt remaining 2 tablespoons butter in skillet over medium heat. Slowly stir flour into the melted butter. Increase heat slowly, stirring and cooking for several minutes, until the flour is well browned. Remove pan from heat and cool slightly.

In saucepan, heat mushroom-butter broth to boiling. Pour broth into butter-flour mixture in skillet. When it stops steaming, stir the mixture briskly with a whisk or large fork. Use a spoon or spatula to scrape the skillet so flour-butter mixture is incorporated into the broth. Put skillet on medium-high heat and let the gravy simmer for several minutes, adding mushroom-onion mixture for the last 2 minutes. Salt and pepper, to taste.

On each of 4 plates, arrange a chuck patty with a portion of mashed potatoes on the side. Pour mushroom-onion gravy over chuck and potatoes. Serve immediately. Serve with sour cream, horseradish sauce, and spicy mustard. Serves 4.

Double Mushroom Meatloaf

Sandra L. Stewart and R. Timothy Haley

Mushrooms star twice in this classic American dish. Make delicious sandwiches with the extras.

1 lb. lean ground beef

½ lb. lean ground sausage

½ lb. ground lamb

1½ cups cooked rice

½ cup onion, finely chopped

½ cup red pepper, finely chopped

2 cups fresh white or brown mushrooms (1 cup finely chopped; 1 cup thinly sliced)

1 tbsp. whole caraway seed

3 cloves minced fresh garlic or 1 tbsp. garlic powder

1 tsp. ground black pepper

1 tbsp. fresh basil

1 tsp. red chile powder

1 can (6 oz.) tomato paste

Juice of 1 lemon

3 oz. water

1 tbsp. soy sauce

In a large bowl, combine beef, sausage, lamb, rice, onion, bell pepper, and chopped mushrooms.

Add caraway seed, garlic, pepper, basil, and chile powder. Mix thoroughly into meat mixture. In a small saucepan, heat tomato paste, lemon juice, water, and soy sauce, stirring on medium-high heat until thick. Cool. Mix half the tomato sauce into the meat mixture. Pack meat loaf into a large loaf pan. Spread remaining sauce on top. Bake at 350 degrees for 1 hour. Carefully pour off fat. Pour sliced mushrooms on top and bake for 10 more minutes. Serves 6-8.

Curried Lamb
with Mushrooms and Wild Rice
Sandra L. Stewart and R. Timothy Haley

A simple, one-dish meal with an exotic flavor of the Middle East. Serve with flat bread and Tabbouleh (salad).

2 tbsp. olive oil

2 lb. lean lamb, cut in 2-inch chunks

½ cup wild rice

½ cup water

1 cup lamb or beef broth

1 tbsp. fresh ginger root, chopped, (or ¼ tsp. ground ginger)

2 tbsp. curry powder

2 cloves garlic, minced

1 small onion, quartered

2 cups white or brown mushrooms, thickly sliced

9 or 10 sprigs of cilantro

In a large, heavy skillet or Dutch oven, heat oil on medium heat. Add the lamb and brown on all sides. Pour off fat and oil. Add rice, water, broth, ginger, curry powder, garlic, and onion. Cover and simmer for 2 hours or until lamb is tender. Add mushrooms. Simmer, covered, for 10 more minutes. Serve in bowls. Garnish with cilantro. Serves 6.

Teriyaki Mushroom Burgers

Courtesy of Monterey Mushrooms, Santa Cruz, California

Use half the mushrooms in the meat; half in the flavorful sauce. 183 calories per serving.

1 egg, slightly beaten

1 tbsp. and 2 tsp. soy sauce

1½ tsp. instant minced onion

¼ tsp. garlic salt

1 lb. fresh white or brown mushrooms

1 lb. lean ground beef

1 tsp. butter or margarine

1 tsp. cornstarch

Combine egg, 1 tablespoon soy sauce, onion, and garlic salt. Let stand 5 minutes.

Finely chop half the mushrooms. Slice remaining half and set aside. Add ground beef and chopped mushrooms to egg mixture. Mix lightly. Shape into 6 patties. Broil to desired doneness. Turn midway. Brush with additional soy sauce.

Meanwhile, sauté remaining sliced mushrooms in butter and 2 tsp. soy sauce about 2 minutes. Sprinkle with cornstarch. Heat and stir 3-4 minutes or until part of liquid has evaporated and mushrooms are coated with thin sauce. Transfer patties to serving platter. Top with mushrooms. Serves 6.

Chicken Chop Suey

Courtesy of Monterey Mushrooms, Santa Cruz, California

Eye-appealing, delicious, and low in calories. 244 calories per serving.

1 chicken bouillon cube

1½ cups water

2 cups bias-cut celery

1 cup thinly-sliced onion

½ lb. fresh white mushrooms, sliced

1 can (16 oz.) bean sprouts, drained

⅓ cup soy sauce

¼ cup cornstarch

2 cups diced cooked chicken

2 tbsp. coarsley chopped pimiento

3 cups hot cooked rice

In a large saucepan, dissolve bouillon cube in boiling water. Add celery and onion. Cover. Cook 5 minutes. Stir in mushrooms. Cover. Cook 5 minutes longer. Add bean sprouts.

In a cup, combine soy sauce and cornstarch until smooth. Add to mushroom mixture. Heat and stir until thickened and clear. Stir in chicken and pimiento. Heat through. Serve over rice. Serves 6.

Italian Mushroom Spaghetti

Courtesy of Monterey Mushrooms, Santa Cruz, California

A thick and saucy vegetarian main dish. 166 calories per serving. (One tablespoon Parmesan cheese equals 21 calories.)

1 can (15 oz.) tomato sauce

1 cup chopped onion

1 clove garlic, minced

1½ tsp. brown sugar

1¼ tsp. seasoned salt

¾ tsp. oregano, crushed

½ bay leaf

1 lb. fresh white or brown mushrooms, thinly sliced

2 tsp. cornstarch

2 tsp. cool water

6 oz. spaghetti, cooked

Parmesan cheese

In a large saucepan, combine tomato sauce, onion, garlic, sugar, salt, oregano, and bay leaf. Heat to boiling. Reduce heat. Cover and simmer 15 minutes, stirring occasionally. Stir in mushrooms. Simmer, covered, 15 minutes longer. Stir occasionally. In a cup, combine cornstarch and water until smooth. Stir into sauce. Heat until slightly thickened. Serve over hot spaghetti. Sprinkle with Parmesan cheese. Serves 6.

Chicken Paprika

Courtesy of Monterey Mushrooms, Santa Cruz, California

A low-calorie version of a popular main dish. 198 calories per serving.

3 chicken breasts, skinned and halved

1 lb. fresh medium white mushrooms, sliced

1 cup chopped onion

1 clove garlic, minced

1 can (8 oz.) tomato sauce

$\frac{1}{4}$ cup water

1 chicken bouillon cube

$4\frac{1}{2}$ tsp. paprika

1 tsp. salt

$\frac{1}{8}$ tsp. pepper

$\frac{1}{2}$ cup dairy sour cream

$\frac{1}{2}$ cup plain lowfat yogurt

2 to $2\frac{1}{2}$ tbsp. cornstarch

Snipped parsley

In baking dish or pan, broil chicken 3 inches from flame, for 8 minutes on each side, or until browned.

In large skillet or Dutch oven combine mushrooms, onion, garlic, tomato sauce, water, bouillon cube, paprika, salt, and pepper. Heat and stir to break up bouillon cube. Add chicken. Cover. Simmer about 30 minutes or until chicken is tender.

In a small bowl, combine sour cream, yogurt, and cornstarch. Remove chicken to serving dish. Keep warm. Stir sour cream mixture into sauce. Heat and stir over low heat just until sauce begins to simmer. Pour over chicken. Sprinkle with snipped parsley. Serves 6.

Saucy Meatball Stroganoff

Courtesy of Monterey Mushrooms, Santa Cruz, California

A delicious way to use ground beef. 214 calories per serving.

2 slices slightly dry white bread, crusts removed

⅓ cup water

⅓ cup onion, finely chopped

1 tsp. seasoned salt

⅛ tsp. pepper

⅛ tsp. ground thyme

1 lb. extra lean ground beef

1 lb. fresh medium, white or brown mushrooms, sliced

1 beef bouillon cube

1 tbsp. cornstarch

½ cup plain lowfat yogurt

¼ cup dairy sour cream

¼ cup snipped parsley

Soak bread in bowl of water about 5 minutes. Squeeze out moisture. In a large bowl, combine soaked bread with onion, salt, pepper, and thyme. Mix in ground beef. Shape into 18 balls, about 1½ inches in diameter. Heat large skillet over medium heat. Add meatballs. Brown 8-10 minutes, shaking pan several times to turn meatballs. Drain on absorbent paper. Keep warm.

Reserve 2 tablespoons pan drippings in skillet. Add mushrooms. Sauté about 5 minutes or until tender. Add bouillon cube. Stir to dissolve in liquid from mushrooms. Sprinkle cornstarch over mushrooms. Stir to coat. Add yogurt and sour cream. Heat slowly until sauce thickens, about 5 minutes. Do not boil. Stir in meatballs and parsley. Serve immediately. Serves 6.

Shrimp Creole

Courtesy of Monterey Mushrooms, Santa Cruz, California

Serve over hot rice. 242 calories per serving.

1 can (16 oz.) tomatoes, broken up

1 clove garlic, minced

1 tsp. sugar

1 tsp. salt

⅛ tsp. pepper

⅛ tsp. curry powder

1 bay leaf

1 lb. fresh medium white mushrooms, sliced

¾ cup onion, coarsely chopped

½ cup green bell pepper, coarsely chopped

12 oz. cleaned, deveined shrimp, cooked

2½ tbsp. cornstarch

2½ tbsp. water

3 cups hot cooked rice

In large saucepan, combine tomatoes, garlic, sugar, salt, pepper, curry powder, and bay leaf. Add mushrooms, onion, and bell pepper. Stir until thoroughly moistened (vegetables cook down when heated). Cook over medium-high heat until vegetables are tender, about 20 minutes, stirring occasionally. Combine cornstarch and water. Stir into vegetables. Add shrimp. Heat and stir just until boiling. Remove bay leaf. Serve over rice. Serves 6.

Polynesian Chicken Thighs with Mushrooms

Sandra L. Stewart and R. Timothy Haley

For a fresh fruit break, try this exotic dish any time of the year.

1 tbsp. molasses

¼ cup low-sodium soy sauce

8 large chicken thighs, skinned and deboned

Ginger fruit sauce

1 cup orange juice

2 tbsp. lemon juice

2 tbsp. low-sodium soy sauce

1 tbsp. cornstarch

1 tbsp. molasses

¼ cup fresh ginger, peeled and diced

1 fresh pineapple, cubed

1 fresh papaya, cubed

3 cups fresh medium, white mushrooms, halved

Prepare chicken

In a large baking dish, mix the molasses with the soy sauce; add the chicken thighs and let stand for 10 minutes, turning thighs over once. Broil chicken thighs 5 inches from flame for 8 minutes on each side. Pour off fat and juices.

Ginger fruit sauce

In a large saucepan, combine orange juice, lemon juice, and molasses. In a small bowl, stir cornstarch into soy sauce until smooth. Add to ingredients in saucepan. Heat and stir entire mixture until thick and bubbly. Remove from heat. Stir in ginger, pineapple, papaya, and mushrooms. Pour sauce over chicken.

Broil for ten minutes longer or until lightly browned on top. Serves 4.

Italian Stuffed Peppers

Sandra L. Stewart and R. Timothy Haley

Mushrooms add a delicate, meaty texture to this classic folk dish.

4 large red or yellow peppers

2 tbsp. olive oil

1 onion, diced

3 cloves garlic, minced

2 cups eggplant, diced

1 tbsp. fresh basil (or 1 tsp. dry)

1 tbsp. fresh oregano (or 1 tsp. dry)

2 cups fresh medium, white or
  brown mushrooms, finely chopped

1 cup cooked brown rice

1 can (6 oz.) tomato paste

1½ cups water

½ cup red wine

4 large slices mozzarella cheese

Cut tops off peppers; remove seeds and membranes. In covered saucepan, boil pepper shells in water at a level half the size of peppers, for 10 minutes or until barely tender.

Heat olive oil in large skillet. Sauté onion, garlic, and eggplant for 5 minutes. Mix in basil, oregano, mushrooms, and rice.

Fill peppers with the mushroom-rice mixture. Arrange them in a baking pan. Spoon extra filling around peppers in pan.

In skillet, combine tomato paste with water. Bring to a boil and stir until thickened. Add wine, stirring, and cook 1 minute more. Pour sauce over peppers and extra stuffing. Bake, uncovered, at 350 degrees for 20 minutes. Place a slice of cheese on top of each pepper; bake 5 minutes longer. Serves 4.

Filets de Soles á la Carmel

Chef Yukio Fukushima, Café Petite Maison, Watsonville, California

A truly inspired gourmet meal that you can order at this gem of a restaurant on central California's coast. Or, make it yourself. The recipe is a culinary gift, graciously given.

½ lb. filet of sole

Salt, to taste

Pepper, to taste

6 fresh small Shiitake mushrooms

1 tbsp. onion, chopped

1 tbsp. fresh tomato, diced

1½ square feet Yuba (soy bean skin, available in Chinese markets)

⅔ cup fish broth

¼ cup white wine

1 pinch saffron

¼ cup whipping cream, unsweetened

Raspberries or blueberries

Salt and pepper fish. Top fish with tomatoes, onion, and 2 chopped Shiitake. Wrap this mixture in Yuba. Place Yuba in the middle of a plate about 1 inch deep. Pour fish broth, wine, and saffron over Yuba. Cover with the 4 remaining Shiitake. Steam for 16 to 18 minutes.

Remove Yuba to plate, reserving the soup and pieces of Shiitake. *Purée the stuffed Yuba and place it on a serving plate. Place Shiitake pieces on top of Yuba mixture.

In a saucepan, heat reserved soup and thicken with whipping cream. Pour over the Yuba and Shiitake. In a circle around the Yuba, garnish the plate with sprigs of fresh basil and raspberries or blueberries. Serves 2.

Do not use an electric blender or food processor. Use a strainer, or preferably, a shinwa.

Lemon-Mushroom Chicken

Sandra L. Stewart and R. Timothy Haley

Enjoy the sunny taste of lemons; this dish has the elements of gourmet cooking, without the fuss. Serve over rice or pasta.

Chicken

3 tbsp. olive oil

3 cloves garlic, chopped

1 medium yellow onion, chopped

1 red bell pepper, cut into strips

1 lb. boneless, skinless, chicken thighs

Juice of 2 medium lemons

Mushroom-Cream sauce

3 tbsp. butter

2 tbsp. flour

1 cup hot milk

1 tsp. chicken bouillon powder

1 dash of white pepper

2 tbsp. white wine

½ lb. fresh medium white mushrooms, sliced thickly

Heat oil on medium-high in large non-stick skillet. Sauté garlic, onion, and bell pepper. Add chicken; sauté lightly until browned, turning once.

In medium saucepan, melt butter. Remove from heat and stir in flour until smooth. Add the milk and stir vigorously until thickened. Mix in bouillon powder, white pepper, and wine.

Pour cream sauce over chicken in skillet. Add mushrooms. Simmer, covered, for 15 minutes or until chicken is cooked through. Serves 4.

Pepper Beef in Shiitake Mushroom Sauce

Azumaya Inc. (Dried Mushrooms), San Francisco, California

In Japan, the Shiitake is a sacred, medicinal food.

1½ oz. dried Shiitake mushrooms

1½ cups hot water

1 tbsp. honey

2 tbsp. soy sauce

1 tsp. dry mustard

2 tsp. cornstarch

1 lb. beef sirloin, sliced thinly, in 2-inch strips

Salt, to taste

Pepper, to taste

2 tbsp. peanut oil

1 medium onion, cut into 1½-inch pieces

1 large green or red bell pepper, cut into 1½-inch pieces

Soak mushrooms in water, to cover, for 30 minutes. Drain. Strain liquid and reserve it. Remove stems from mushrooms and cut mushroom caps in half.

In small saucepan, combine honey, soy sauce, mustard, cornstarch, and 1 cup of cooled mushroom liquid. Stir to dissolve all ingredients. Bring to a boil. Reduce heat; simmer sauce 5 to 7 minutes until thick and velvety. Mix in sliced mushrooms and remove pan from heat.

Sprinkle raw beef with salt and pepper. Pre-heat 1 tablespoon peanut oil on high, in wok or skillet. Quickly sauté beef strips for 1 minute on each side. Remove beef from wok to warm platter. Add remaining peanut oil to wok and sauté onion and bell pepper until onion becomes translucent (about 7 minutes). Stir in beef. Pour mushroom mixture over beef mixture. Toss thoroughly; simmer, covered, for 5 minutes. Serve immediately. Serves 4-6.

Fettucine with Oyster Mushrooms and Broccoli

Sandra L. Stewart and R. Timothy Haley

So fresh and slighty chewy. A colorful example of California cuisine.

1 tbsp. olive oil

3 large shallots, minced

½ lb. fresh Oyster mushrooms, torn in large pieces

3 cloves garlic, minced

3 tbsp. red wine

2 or 3 tsp. soy sauce

1 tsp. dried thyme

1 tsp. dried rosemary

1 small bunch broccoli, cut into small flowerets

¾ lb. whole wheat or semolina fettucine

½ cup fresh Parmesan cheese, grated

10 cups water

Heal oil in large skillet or wok. Add shallots and sauté until softened. Stir in mushroom pieces; sauté for 5 minutes, turning. Remove mushroom-shallot mixture to a bowl; set aside.

In skillet or wok, combine garlic, wine, soy sauce, thyme, and rosemary. Add broccoli. Cook, covered, for 7 minutes. Stir in mushroom-shallot mixture and simmer, covered, 2 minutes longer.

In large saucepan, boil fettucine in water until *al dente*. Drain thoroughly in colander, tossing with a fork. Pour fettucine on a large serving platter. Add mushroom-broccoli sauce and toss until fettucine is coated with sauce. Serves 4.

Cook pasta until barely tender; still a bit firm.

Oyster Mushroom
Pleurotus ostreatu

Brown Mushroom, Eggplant, and Caper Lasagne
Sandra L. Stewart and R. Timothy Haley

This vegetarian meal deserves the stronger, richer flavor of brown mushrooms. If brown mushrooms are unavailable, substitute white mushrooms.

11½ cups water

7 to 8 extra-wide lasagne noodles

3 tbsp. olive oil

2 large Japanese eggplants, thinly sliced, lengthwise

4 cloves garlic, minced

1 cup onion, chopped

1 cup red bell pepper, chopped

4 cups fresh brown mushrooms, thickly sliced

1 can (6 oz.) tomato paste

1 tbsp. fresh oregano, chopped (or 1 tsp. powdered)

2 tbsp. fresh basil (or 1 tsp. dried)

2 tsp. black pepper

1 carton (15 oz.) ricotta cheese

2 cups mozzarella cheese, shredded

1 (4 oz.) jar capers, drained

In a large pot, bring 10 cups water to boil. Add lasagne noodles and boil on medium heat for about 20 minutes or until *al dente*. Pour noodles into colander to drain and cool.

Heat 1 tablespoon oil in a large skillet. Sauté eggplant on medium heat for 15 minutes or until softened, turning once. Remove eggplant from pan and set aside.

Heat a second tablespoon oil in skillet. On medium heat, sauté garlic, onion, bell pepper, and mushrooms, stirring, for 10 minutes. Remove pan from heat. Stir in tomato paste and 1½ cups water. Add oregano, basil, and black pepper. Simmer sauce for 10 minutes, covered, or until thickened.

Spread a thin layer of sauce on bottom of 9x14x2-inch dish or pan. Cover with half the lasagne noodles. Over the noodles, layer eggplant, ricotta cheese, mozzarella cheese, half the capers, and half the mushroom sauce. Lay on second layer of noodles, remaining capers, and remaining mushroom sauce. Sprinkle with remaining mozzarella cheese.

Bake uncovered at 350 degrees for 30 minutes. Cool slightly before serving. Serves 6-8.

Shiitake Foil

Chef Yukio Fukushima, Café Petite Maison, Watsonville, California

Nouvelle Cuisine from one of the South Bay's wonderful restaurants.

3 fresh Shiitake mushrooms

1 lb. sea bass filet

1½ tsp. butter

Salt, to taste

Pepper, to taste

2 tbsp. white wine

2 tbsp. low sodium soy sauce

1½ square feet of tin foil

Trim stems from Shiitake. Rinse them and cut in halves or quarters. Smear butter in center of foil. Place sea bass on top of butter. Put Shiitake pieces on top of sea bass. Add salt, pepper, and wine. Sprinkle soy sauce on Shiitake and sea bass. Wrap loosely in foil, sealed well. Broil foil package under medium heat for 8 minutes. Garnish with lemon wedges. Serves 2.

Shiitake with Ahi Tuna

Sandra L. Stewart and R. Timothy Haley

These natural gifts from the forest and sea rival each other for strength and richness in a bold sauce.

1 lb. Ahi tuna fillet, cut in half

⅔ cup soy sauce

5 dried Shiitake mushrooms

½ cup hot water

2 to 3 tbsp. peanut or olive oil

1 clove garlic, pressed or minced

2 tbsp. shredded, fresh ginger root

1 red onion, cut into thin wedges

5 tbsp. dry sherry

1½ tsp. cornstarch

1 tsp. sugar

Black or Szechuan pepper to taste

1 tbsp. sesame seeds, toasted*

cilantro sprigs

*To toast, spread sesame seeds on a cookie sheet or pie pan. Bake at 450 degrees for 7 minutes.

In a medium bowl, place Ahi fillets in soy sauce, turning once. Set aside.

Place Shiitake mushrooms in a small bowl. Cover with hot water and let soak 20 minutes. Drain, reserving soaking liquid. Rinse Shiitake well. Trim off tough stems and slice caps into large pieces. Set aside.

Remove Ahi fillet from marinade, reserving liquid. On a rack in the oven, broil the fillet for 7 or 8 minutes on each side or until center is slightly flaky.

In a wok or medium skillet, heat oil over high heat. Add garlic, ginger, and onion to wok and stir-fry 2 minutes. Add Shiitake and stir-fry 1 minute. Pour in soy sauce marinade and soaking liquid from Shiitake.

In a small bowl, blend sherry, cornstarch, and sugar, stirring until thickened and smooth. Add sherry mixture to Shiitake mixture. Season with pepper and simmer for 2 minutes.

Place filets on two plates. Cover each fillet with half the sauce. Garnish with sesame seeds and cilantro sprigs. Serves 2.

Mushroom and Chicken Morocco with Olives

Sandra L. Stewart and R. Timothy Haley

Soul food to warm the home and heart. Time is of no consequence when preparing this Moroccan main dish, simmered at length. Serve with rice and crusty bread.

2 tbsp. olive oil

1 3 lb. whole chicken

1 tsp. ground cumin

1 tsp. ground ginger

1 tbsp. sweet paprika

⅛ tsp. Spanish saffron* powder or crushed threads

Juice of 1 lemon

2 cloves garlic, minced

1 cup water or chicken broth plus additional water for boiling olives

2 cups fresh white or brown mushrooms, chopped into large, irregular pieces

10 oz. green, pitted, low-salt olives, rinsed and drained

Freshly ground pepper

Buy Spanish saffron powder or threads in gourmet supermarkets or specialty stores.

Heat oil in Dutch oven over medium heat. Add whole chicken and brown on all sides. Spoon off fat. Add cumin, ginger, paprika, saffron, lemon juice, garlic, and one cup water or chicken broth. Cover and cook over medium-low heat until chicken is tender, about 1½ hours. Remove from heat. Add mushrooms.

Bring ½ cup water to boil in small saucepan. Add drained olives and boil 5 minutes. Drain again and crush olives with fork. Add to chicken and mushrooms and cook 10 minutes longer over medium-low heat. Season to taste with pepper.

Serves 6.

Cous Cous with Fresh Shiitake and Chicken

Sandra L. Stewart and R. Timothy Haley

Soothe your family's spirits with this comfort food from Morocco. Shiitake imbue this dish with the meditative traditions of China, as well. In California, instant cous cous is marketed as "Moroccan pasta," and commonly found on supermarket shelves in Middle Eastern markets, or in health food stores.

2 tbsp. olive oil

1 fryer chicken (3-lb.), cut into pieces

1 medium onion, sliced

6 cups water

1 bunch cilantro, rinsed and tied with string

1 tsp. saffron powder or crushed saffron threads

3 tsp. turmeric

Salt, to taste

Pepper, to taste

6 fresh large Shiitake mushrooms, stems removed, quartered

1 cup raisins

4 tbsp. butter or margarine

2 tsp. cinnamon

2 tsp. ground ginger

2 tbsp. slivered almonds

¼ cup honey

1 lb. instant cous cous grain

Heat the oil in a large soup pot. Brown the chicken and add 1 cup sliced onions. Reserve the remaining onions. Add the water, tied cilantro, saffron, 1 teaspoon turmeric, and salt and pepper to taste. Cover and bring to a boil; then lower the heat and cook until chicken is tender (about 45 minutes). Discard the cilantro. Skim off fat from broth. Add Shiitake; cover and reduce heat. Simmer the chicken and mushrooms until very tender (another 20 minutes).

Soak the raisins in warm water for about ½ hour. Drain.

In a frying pan, sauté the remaining onions in butter or margarine. Add the cinnamon, ginger, almonds, honey, and raisins. Cover and cook over low heat for 25 minutes. Set aside.

To cook the cous cous grain, proceed as directed on the package.

To serve, place the cous cous in a large bowl, spoon a little broth over the grain and fluff with a fork. Pack the cous cous tightly down in the bowl and set the bowl on a serving platter. With a large spoon, make a well in the center of the mound of cous cous. Tuck the warm chicken and mushroom pieces inside the well. Cover with the sweet onion and raisin mixture. Serve with extra broth on the side. Serves 4-6.

Oyster Mushrooms and Scallops in Lemon Caper Sauce

Sandra L. Stewart and R. Timothy Haley

"Fish" from the woods (cultivated Oyster mushrooms) and jewels of the sea pair up for a light and beautiful main dish.

1 tbsp. olive oil

1 lb. fresh sea scallops

2 cloves garlic, minced

2 tbsp. onion, finely chopped

½ cup fresh lemon juice, strained

5 fresh large Oyster mushrooms torn in bite-sized pieces

2 tbsp. capers

Heat oil in skillet on medium-high heat. Sauté scallops for 8 minutes, turning once. Remove from pan with slotted spoon or spatula; set aside. To fish-butter broth in pan, add garlic, onion, and lemon juice. Sauté, stirring, for 5 minutes. Add mushroom pieces and continue cooking for 5 more minutes. Stir in capers and add pre-cooked scallops to the sauce. Cover and simmer for 7 minutes or until all ingredients are hot. Serve immediately in small bowls. Serves 4.

Mushrooms St. Jacques

Joan Jones, Favorite Recipe Contest Finalist,
Morgan Hill's Mushroom Mardi Gras

A French classic, sharpened with cheddar cheese for the American palate.

2 tbsp. butter

1 cup milk

1½ to 2 tbsp. flour

1 egg yolk

2 tbsp. cream

1½ large onions, finely chopped

2 stalks celery, finely chopped

1½ lb. fresh small white mushrooms, sliced (sautéed in butter and strained)

6 oz. fresh shrimp or crab meat, lightly cooked

2 tbsp. grated Parmesan cheese

2 or 3 tbsp. Cheddar cheese, finely grated

6 or 8 seafood shells*

Buy seafood shells for stuffing at your favorite, well-stocked "kitchen" store.

Melt butter in a small saucepan. Add a little milk to the flour to make a thin paste. In a large saucepan, heat remaining milk. Add the flour paste to the milk. Cook slowly till thickened, stirring constantly.

Add onions, celery, and sautéed mushrooms; bring to a boil, stirring constantly for about 1 minute.

In a bowl, beat egg yolk and cream together until blended. Add a little of the flour sauce to the egg mixture, stirring constantly. Pour the remaining egg-cream mixture into the flour-vegetable sauce; slowly heat thoroughly. Do not boil.

Add the shrimp or crab meat, Parmesan, and Cheddar cheeses; stir thoroughly.

Spoon into seafood shells. Top shells with Parmesan cheese. Broil 5 inches from heat until the tops take on a delicate color. Serves 3 or 4.

Mary's Mushroom Soufflé
Mary Hiller

Light and elegant with plenty of mushroom flavor.

5 eggs

1 lb. white mushrooms, thinly sliced and sautéed until soft

2 tbsp. butter

3 tbsp. flour

½ tsp. salt

1 tsp. cayenne pepper

¼ tsp. nutmeg

Separate eggs, putting egg whites into a medium bowl. Drain mushrooms through a sieve, reserving broth. Dry mushrooms with a paper towel. Chop finely until almost puréed. Add reserved mushroom liquid back to puréed mushrooms. Melt butter and add flour; then add mushroom mixture, salt, pepper, and nutmeg. Cook in a non-stick skillet over low heat until thickened. Beat egg yolks slightly and blend into hot mushroom mixture. Remove from heat and cool. Beat egg whites until stiff. Lightly fold into mushroom-egg mixture. Pour into ungreased 6-cup soufflé pan. Bake at 350 degrees for 30 to 35 minutes, until golden brown. Serve immediately. Serves 4-6.

Italian Mushroom Casserole

Molly M. Martin, Favorite Recipe Contest Finalist,
Morgan Hill's Mushroom Mardi Gras

An authentic Italian dish that features the stunning combination of
mushrooms and eggplant.

Casserole
2 tbsp. butter
¼ tsp. dried basil
½ tsp. dried thyme
½ tsp. dried oregano
1 clove garlic, crushed
¼ tsp. paprika
¼ tsp. rosemary
1½ lb. fresh medium, white or
  brown mushrooms, whole
Salt, to taste
Pepper, to taste
3-4 oz. Parmesan cheese, grated
1 quart Eggplant Sauce

Eggplant Sauce
½ cup olive oil
2 or 3 cloves garlic, minced
1 medium eggplant (about 1 lb.), peeled
  and chopped
2 green bell peppers
½ to ¾ cup sliced black olives
3 to 4 tbsp. capers
1 tsp. crushed basil
Salt, to taste
Fresh ground pepper, to taste
3 cups peeled and chopped tomatoes*
12 oz. tomato paste
2 cups dry wine (more if needed)

*To easily peel, put tomato into boiling water for
2 or 3 minutes. Cool; then peel.

Melt the butter in a large skillet; add the basil, thyme, oregano, garlic, paprika, and rosemary. Add mushrooms for 10 minutes or until tender. Stir occasionally to evenly distribute herbs over the mushrooms. Add salt and pepper to taste.

Arrange mushrooms in an even layer in a buttered medium-sized baking dish. Sprinkle Parmesan cheese on mushrooms. Carefully pour Eggplant Sauce over cheese, spreading it evenly. Cover dish and bake at 350 degrees for 15 minutes, or until hot throughout.

Eggplant Sauce
Heat olive oil in large skillet. Add garlic; let it heat gently while you prepare vegetables.

Add eggplant, peppers, olives, and capers to oil. Stir well. Add basil, salt, pepper, tomatoes, tomato paste, and wine.

Lower heat. Simmer sauce gently for 1 hour. Stir occasionally to avoid scorching. Add more wine if sauce is too thick. Makes about 2 quarts.

Morgan Hill Mushrooms Magnifique

Nancy Jolin, Morgan Hill's Mushroom Mardi Gras Cookoff Finalist

A simple, pasta dish, teeming with fresh mushrooms and shrimp.

2 cloves garlic, minced

1 lb. fresh medium white mushrooms, sliced

1 cube butter

1 lb. fresh small shrimp

Salt, to taste

Pepper, to taste

7 or 8 oz. dry noodles

In a non-stick skillet, sauté garlic and mushrooms in butter. Add shrimp, salt, and pepper. Cook until shrimp are done, about 10 minutes. Cook noodles according to package directions. Drain; pour onto serving platter. Add mushroom and shrimp combination to noodles. Blend together and serve. Serves 4.

A Gringo's Version Of Mexican Pasta

Jayne Chick, Morgan Hill's Mushroom Mardi Gras Cookoff Finalist

Tortillas stand in for pasta in this south-of-the-border dish. Serve in a colorful Mexican clay casserole.

12 corn tortillas

5 chicken half breasts, boned and skinned

8 dry *ancho* chilies (mild California chilies)

1 small green chili (hot)

2 cloves garlic

1 tsp. oregano

4 fresh tomatoes, peeled and quartered

1 cup chicken stock

2 tbsp. vegetable oil

Salt, to taste

Pepper, to taste

1 lb. mushrooms, thickly sliced

2 onions (cut in half; cut halves into half-rings)

1 cup sharp cheddar cheese, grated

Sour cream

Avocado

Cilantro sprigs

Cut tortillas into strips and spread on cookie sheet. Bake 20-25 minutes at 325 degrees until crisp and golden.

Place chicken in a saucepan with enough water to cover. Bring to boil; then turn heat down and simmer 1 hour or until chicken is tender. Cool, strain, and save stock. Cut chicken into large chunks. Set aside.

Remove stems, seeds, and veins from the ancho chilies. Place in saucepan and cover with boiling water. Boil 10 minutes. Remove from heat and allow to soak for 1 hour. Drain. Place chilies in blender with hot green chili, garlic, oregano, tomatoes, and chicken stock.

Heat 2 tablespoons oil in heavy saucepan and fry the chili sauce for 2 minutes, stirring constantly. Lower the heat and simmer 10 minutes. Add salt and pepper.

Heat remaining 2 tablespoons oil in large frying pan. Add mushrooms and onions and cook, stirring gently until soft. Add the chili mixture and chicken; cook together for 5 minutes. Stir in the tortilla strips and heat through. Remove from heat. Stir in the cheese and serve immediately.

If desired, turn into Mexican clay casserole. Serve with sour cream, grated cheese, avocado, and cilantro.

Mushroom El Toro

Barbara Bayless, Morgan Hill's Mushroom Mardi Gras Cookoff Finalist

Think of Morgan Hill's famous mountain while you prepare and eat this uniquely central California dish.

½ lb. fresh medium, white or brown mushrooms

2 tbsp. white wine

1 can (14 oz.) artichoke hearts, drained and cut in chunks

¼ lb. bacon, cooked, drained, and crumbled

2 cans (8 oz. each) tomato sauce

2 tbsp. green onions, chopped

1 small clove garlic

3 tbsp. coarsely chopped walnuts

2 tbsp. chopped parsley

¼ cup grated Romano cheese

With a small paring knife, remove stems from mushrooms. Chop the stems and set aside.

Butter a shallow baking dish. Arrange the mushroom caps and artichoke hearts in layers in the dish. Pour in white wine. Sprinkle bacon over mushrooms and artichokes. Combine tomato sauce, mushroom stems, onions, garlic, walnuts; mix well. Pour over mushroom mixture. Add parsley and cheese. Bake at 350 degrees for 30 minutes. Serves 4.

Fresh Calf Liver and Bacon with Mushroom Stroganoff Sauce

A wonderful "new" old recipe from two great families.

Sandra's dad, Loren Stewart, grew up with eleven brothers and sisters on a Kansas livestock ranch. His dad and uncle were respected cattlemen. Loren's mother and sisters (and brother, Roland, who later became a professional chef-nutritionist) cooked everything "from scratch." They had to. Because of Arthur and Minerva Stewart's resourcefulness, their children and many other American families had enough fresh, protein-rich food to eat during the depression.

Nowadays, Loren and his wife, Peggy, rarely cook liver at home. They eat it at Ryan's Place, a restaurant a few blocks from their home in Porterville, California. The chefs there will cook the liver to any stage of doneness desired.

The calf liver Loren ate as a boy on the ranch was "same-day" fresh. He recommends that you check with your supermarket's butcher to make sure your choice of liver is high quality meat and as fresh as possible.

Fried Calf Liver
Loren and Peggy Stewart

6 slices bacon

3 tbsp. butter or margarine

1 lb. fresh calf liver, cut in half-inch slices

3 tbsp. flour

Salt, to taste

Pepper, to taste

In a large, heavy skillet, fry bacon until crisp, turning once. Remove from pan to a warm plate lined with a paper towel. Carefully scrape fat from pan, leaving fried bacon bits. Return skillet to medium-high heat and melt butter; with a wide spatula, scrape the bacon bits into the butter.

Remove membrane from each slice of liver. Snip out veins with kitchen scissors. Sprinkle liver slices with salt and pepper; dredge in flour. Fry in the hot butter until brown, turning once, for 5 or 6 minutes (for medium doneness). Arrange liver slices on 4 warm plates.

Pour equal portions of Mushroom Stroganoff Sauce (recipe follows) on liver. Garnish each serving with 2 strips of crisp bacon. Serve immediately. Serves 4.

Mushroom Stroganoff Sauce
Connie Hill

One of the Hill family's favorite recipes. From the food stains and fingerprints on the old handwritten recipe card, we know Connie loved to cook this one. She had a note to herself in the upper left-hand corner: "very good."

1 tbsp. margarine or butter

1 large onion, finely chopped

½ lb. fresh white or brown mushrooms, thinly sliced

1 tbsp. flour

¼ cup cool water

2 tbsp. chili sauce (or catsup)

¾ cup regular strength beef broth

2 tbsp. sherry

½ cup sour cream

2 tbsp. chopped parsley

In large skillet, melt butter. Add onion; sauté on medium-high heat, stirring, for 5 minutes. Add mushrooms and sauté 5 minutes longer. Remove skillet from heat. In a cup, mix flour and water with a fork, until smooth; stir into onion-mushroom mixture. Return skillet to medium-high heat. Cook, stirring, for 1 minute. Add chili sauce, broth, and sherry; cook for 5 minutes or until thickened. Stir in sour cream and parsley. Serve hot over Fried Calf Liver. Serves 4.

Chicken And Mushroom Crepes

Renée Spencer, Favorite Recipe Contest,
Morgan Hill's Mushroom Mardi Gras

Creamy cheeses and mushrooms are excellent with chicken in this "dressy" main dish.

5 boneless chicken breasts

1 medium onion

1 lb. fresh mushrooms

3 tbsp. margarine

¼ lb. each shredded mozzarella and swiss cheese

2 cans cream of chicken soup

⅔ cup Parmesan cheese

2 pkg. (6 each) frozen crepes, thawed

Cut chicken breasts into ½-inch cubes; set aside. Chop onion into large coarse pieces, approximately ½ inch. Slice mushrooms into thick pieces. In large 3 quart saucepan, sauté onion in margarine until transparent. Add chicken and cook until tender. Add mushrooms and stir. Cook 5 minutes; add soup and Parmesan cheese; stir. Cover and keep warm.

Fill crepes with approximately ½ cup of filling. Fold crepe and sprinkle mozzarella and Swiss cheese over the top. Bake in a greased 9x13 inch pan at 350 degrees for 20 minutes. Serve while still hot. Makes 12 crepes.

Burgundy Burgers
Connie Hill

George Hill, Jr. remembers his mom's burgers as his favorite childhood mushroom dish.

Burgers

2 lbs ground beef

1 cup soft bread crumbs

1 egg

¼ cup red wine

2 tbsp. sliced green onion

1 tsp. salt

Pepper, to taste

6 French bread slices, toasted

Mushroom Burgundy Sauce

½ cup margarine

2 tbsp. green onion

2 cups fresh white or brown mushrooms, thickly sliced

¼ cup red wine

Burgers

In a bowl, combine beef, bread crumbs, egg, wine, green onion, salt, and pepper. Form into 6 patties. BBQ or broil 5 inches from heat in broiler for 10 minutes, turning once. Place toasted bread slices on 6 plates. Top with burgers. Pour Mushroom Burgundy Sauce over burgers. Serves 6.

Mushroom Burgundy Sauce

In a small skillet, melt butter. Sauté green onions and mushrooms for 7 minutes. Add wine. Simmer for 2 minutes longer.

Chicken Livers Deluxe

Connie Hill

A pound of chicken livers stretches to serve four in this entree. The livers are sautéed and simmered with fresh mushrooms and vegetables.

1 lb. chicken livers

½ cup flour

1 tsp. salt

¼ tsp. pepper

1 medium red onion, sliced

2 cups fresh mushrooms, quartered

1 cup celery, sliced

3 tbsp. butter

3 tbsp. oil

1 clove garlic, pressed

2 cups water

1 tsp. thyme, crumbled

Hot fluffy rice

Wash chicken livers; pat dry. Combine flour, salt, and pepper in plastic bag. Add chicken livers. Shake bag coat to livers with flour. Set aside.

Sauté onion, mushrooms, and celery in 2 tablespoons butter until onion is soft. Remove from skillet. Add remaining butter and oil. Sauté chicken livers with garlic on all sides until browned. Add water and thyme. Simmer, uncovered, 10 minutes.

Stir in sautéed mushrooms and vegetables. Serve with hot, fluffy rice. Serves 4.

Roast Venison with Mushrooms
Connie Hill

Imagine graceful deer racing across the heathered highlands of Scotland. Sweet-tart Cumberland Sauce complements the robust flavor of this venison and Shiitake dish. Rice pilaf is a perfect accompaniment. Listen to a lively tune of bagpipes while you eat.

Roast Venison

1 cup water

1 onion, sliced

2 carrots, sliced

1 tsp. whole peppercorns

1 bay leaf

1½ cups red wine

6 or 7 lbs. venison, rump or saddle

6 or 7 slices bacon

Clusters of green grapes

Cumberland Sauce

2 oz. dried Shiitake mushrooms

2 cups hot water

¼ cup marinade from roast venison, strained

¼ cup broth from mushroom soaking liquid

2 tbsp lemon juice

½ tsp. ginger

4 tbsp. Scotch whiskey

2 cups currant jelly

Roast Venison

In small saucepan, combine water, onion, carrots, peppercorns, and bay leaf. Boil 15 minutes. Add wine and pour hot over meat in large bowl. Let stand in refrigerator overnight or up to 3 days, turning meat occasionally.

Remove meat from marinade; wipe dry. Place roast on a rack in an open pan; lay bacon over top of roast. Roast at 350 degrees for 1½ hours.

Drain vegetables from marinade and place in pan with meat. Baste meat with marinade. Return to oven; roast 1 hour longer. Baste occasionally with marinade. Venison should be rare. Remove to warm platter. Garnish with grape clusters. Serve with Cumberland Sauce. Serves 10-12.

Cumberland Sauce

In a bowl, soak mushrooms in water for 30 minutes. Set aside, reserving broth. In a small saucepan, combine marinade, mushroom broth, currant jelly, lemon juice, ginger, and whiskey. Bring to boil and add mushrooms. Reduce heat; simmer 5 minutes, stirring occasionally. Serves 10-12.

Strive for a marriage (but not a compromise!)
 between elegance and simplicity.
Successful mushroom cookery doesn't
require exotic foods or a
 bottomless bank account or
 idle afternoons or a deep degree in
 gastronomic mechanics. It does require
 patience, sensitivity, enthusiasm, and imagination.
There are no rigorous rules....

Rosetta Reitz, *Mushroom Cookery*

Convenient Recipes

Morgan Hill City Council's Marinated Mushrooms

Courtesy of Beth Wyman, Former Mayor, City of Morgan Hill

A tangy, easy-to-make-ahead appetizer, generous enough to satisfy all your guests.

3 lbs. fresh small white mushrooms
1 16 oz. bottle Italian salad dressing
1 8 oz. bottle red wine salad dressing
¼ tsp. lemon juice

Combine dressings and lemon juice in blender until pink and foamy. Pour over bowl of mushrooms and stir until all mushrooms have been coated. Marinate mushrooms overnight. Stir several times in the morning. Pour off excess marinade before serving. Serves 12-15.

Snow-Capped Mushrooms

Debra Vadalma, Favorite Recipe Contest,
Morgan Hill's Mushroom Mardi Gras

A festival-sized recipe for a quick, tasty, make-ahead appetizer. Simply halve or quarter ingredients for smaller portions. Better yet, freeze a large supply for even more convenience later.

40 fresh medium white mushrooms
1 pkg. (8 oz.) cream cheese, softened
¾ cup Parmesan cheese, finely
  grated
2 tbsp. chives, chopped
5 tbsp. milk
¾ cup butter, softened
½ tsp. garlic powder

With a small paring knife, remove stems from mushrooms. (Reserve stems to use in soup stock for another meal.)

In a large bowl, thoroughly combine cheeses, chives, milk, butter, and garlic powder. Arrange mushroom caps in a baking dish; stuff each cap with cheese mixture. Bake 15 minutes at 350 degrees. If frozen, bake 25 minutes at 375 degrees. Serves 18-20.

Stuffed Potato-Mushroom Casserole

Darlene and Loyd Anderson

Sandra's sister is a teacher at the award-winning West Putnam Elementary School where all five Stewart sisters went to school, in Porterville, California. Darlene and her San Joaquin Valley farmer-husband know how to add a mushroom "punch" to fresh mashed potatoes. Their two teenagers can't get enough of this side dish.

5 large red potatoes, peeled

1 cube butter or margarine

4 green onions, chopped

½ cup sour cream

1 cup sharp cheddar cheese, grated

1 can cream of mushroom soup (do not add water)

In a large saucepan, boil whole potatoes, covered, on medium heat for about 45 minutes or until done. Drain thoroughly. Cut potatoes into pieces, in pan. Put butter in the hot potato pieces. With an electric mixer, mash potatoes and butter. Stir in onions, sour cream, cheese, and soup. Pour mixture into a medium-sized casserole dish. Bake, uncovered, at 350 degrees for 20 minutes. Remove from oven. Stir casserole and serve immediately. Serves 6-8.

Green Bean Casserole

Betty and Hank Haley

Timothy's folks' easy version of a favorite American side dish.

2 cans (1 lb. each) green beans, drained

¾ cup milk

1 can mushroom soup

⅛ tsp. black pepper

1 can (2.8 oz.) French-fried onion rings

In a large bowl, combine beans, milk, soup, pepper, and ½ can onion rings. Pour into medium-sized casserole dish. Bake, uncovered, at 350 degrees for 30 minutes. Top with remaining onions and bake 5 minutes longer. Serves 4-6.

Corn Rarebit
Karen King

Karen has been cooking this recipe for about 18 years, changing it by using different kinds of soup, cheese, or bell pepper. It's very attractive. In her Morgan Hill country kitchen, she makes toast, cuts it into small pieces and pours the rarebit over it. Her husband takes it to work for lunch and warms it in the microwave before eating.

1 can cream of mushroom soup

¼ cup green bell pepper, finely chopped

¼ cup onion, finely chopped

½ lb. cheddar cheese, shredded

2 cups corn

In a medium saucepan, heat soup with pepper, onion, and cheese over low heat until cheese is melted. Add corn and continue cooking until mixture is very hot. Serve on toast. Serves 2-4.

Herbed Chicken
Karen King

What you "have on hand" turns into a tasty dinner.

2 whole chicken breasts, split

Vegetable cooking spray

½ tsp. dried thyme or rosemary

½ tsp. pepper

1 can cream of mushroom soup

¼ cup water

Remove skin from chicken. Spray a 12x8 inch baking dish with vegetable spray. Arrange chicken, breast side up, in dish. Sprinkle with thyme or rosemary and pepper. In a saucepan combine soup and water. Heat and stir for 2 or 3 minutes. Spoon mushroom soup and water mixture over chicken. Cover baking dish with foil. Bake at 350 degrees for 25 minutes or until chicken is fork tender. Remove foil. Bake for 25 minutes longer. Stir sauce before serving. Serves 4.

Chicken Casserole Supreme

Karen King

An easy main dish with plenty of rich, creamy flavor and texture.

3 whole chicken breasts

6 cups water

½ cup celery

½ cup onion

Salt, to taste

Pepper, to taste

1 container (16 oz.) sour cream

1 can cream of mushroom soup

1 package (8 oz.) herb-seasoned stuffing mix

¼ lb. butter, melted

1 cup chicken broth

In a medium-sized covered pot, stew chicken breasts in water on low heat until meat falls from bone. Add celery, onion, salt, and pepper for the last ten minutes of stewing. Cube chicken breasts and mix with sour cream and soup. Pour mixture into 2-quart casserole dish. Mix together stuffing mix, butter, and broth. Spoon on top of chicken. Bake, uncovered, at 350 degrees for 45 minutes. Serves 4.

Rice Casserole

Betty and Hank Haley

Nothing this tasty could be easier.

1 onion, chopped

1 cube butter

1 cup cooked rice

1 can beef consommé

1 can cream of mushroom soup

1 can sliced mushrooms

½ cup water

In a large, non-stick skillet, melt butter and sauté onion and rice on medium-high heat until lightly browned, stirring frequently. In a large casserole dish, combine onion-rice mixture, beef consommé, cream of mushroom soup, sliced mushrooms, and water until thoroughly mixed. Bake, uncovered, at 350 degrees for 1 hour. Serves 6-8.

Change-of-Pace Tacos
Courtesy of Monterey Mushrooms, Santa Cruz, California

Try a mushroom filling instead of meat. 188 calories per serving.

¼ cup taco sauce

¼ cup onion, chopped

1 tbsp. green pepper, chopped

¼ tsp. salt

2 tsp. cornstarch

½ lb. fresh medium white
  mushrooms, chopped

8 ready-to-heat taco shells

3 oz. finely shredded diet
  pasteurized process cheese product

Shredded lettuce

Diced tomato, salted

Combine taco sauce, onion, green pepper, and salt in medium-sized saucepan. Bring to boil. Reduce heat. Cover and simmer about 5 minutes, stirring occasionally. Toss cornstarch with mushrooms. Stir into sauce. Simmer, uncovered, 8 minutes or until mushrooms are tender and sauce is thick. Stir occasionally.

Meanwhile, heat taco shells according to package directions. Spoon 2 tablespoons mushroom mixture into each shell. Top with 2 tablespoons diet cheese product. Repeat for remaining tacos. Add lettuce and tomato as desired. Serves 4.

Salad Delicious

Mary Van Walkenburg, Morgan Hill's
Mushroom Mardi Gras Cookoff

If you need a large, make-ahead salad, this one will serve a potluck or small banquet. Try Oyster mushrooms for a surprise gourmet touch.

1 lb. fresh spinach (torn into bite sized pieces)

1 lb. fresh, white (sliced) or Oyster (torn) mushrooms

6 hard boiled eggs, chopped

1 head iceberg lettuce

1 bunch green onions, chopped

½ lb. crisp fried bacon, crumbled

1 cup celery, chopped

Dressing

1 pkg. Ranch-style salad dressing

1 cup sour cream

2 cups mayonnaise

½ cup buttermilk

Toss all ingredients in a large bowl and spread dressing on top, like frosting. Refrigerate 6-8 hours. Toss and serve. Serves 15-20.

Merilyn's Russian stroganoff
Merilyn Meredith

Merilyn got this recipe from a Russian-born American air force sergeant when Hap, Merilyn's husband, was overseas in the military. Merilyn was unable to cook for a few days because of an injury. The air force sergeant took pity on Merilyn and her kids and invited them over for supper. The sergeant cooked this Russian-American specialty. Since that time, Merilyn says, "It's been a favorite of all my kids, too."

1 large round steak, cut into strips

1 large onion, chopped

1 clove garlic, chopped, or 1 tbsp. garlic powder

2 tbsp. vegetable oil

1 can tomato soup

½ can water

¼ lb. fresh large, white or brown mushrooms, sliced

½ pint sour cream

Salt, to taste

Pepper, to taste

Brown steak strips and onions in oil. Add garlic, soup, and water. Simmer until meat is tender (about 1 hour). Add the mushrooms. Heat and stir until hot. Add sour cream, salt, and pepper. Mix and stir over heat until hot. Serve over noodles or rice. Serves 6.

Betos' Mushroom Brunch

Alberto Hoff, Morgan Hill's Mushroom Mardi Gras Cookoff

Tired of sandwiches? Try this quick, easy meal. Kids love it.

½ lb. fresh medium white mushrooms, thinly sliced

½ cup butter

½ medium onion

1 tbsp. flour

1 cup cold milk

The juice of half orange

½ tbsp. parsley

Salt, to taste

Pepper, to taste

4 slices of toast rounds

4 slices of turkey ham

1 can (4 slices) pineapple

With a small paring knife, remove stems from mushrooms; chop finely. Melt butter and sauté mushroom stems and slices with onion for 8 minutes. In a jar, mix flour and milk; add to mushrooms. Cook until creamy. Add the orange juice and parsley. Season with salt and pepper to taste.

Place toast rounds in a baking dish; top each round with a thin slice of turkey ham. Top each slice ham with 1 slice pineapple. Cover with mushroom mixture. Heat at 350 degrees for 10 minutes. Serve immediately. Serves 4.

The World's largest living thing may not be a California redwood tree but a vast fungus whose underground tendrils extend across nearly 40 acres in a Michigan forest.

The monster fungus seems to be all one individual organism, not a colony as previously supposed. . . The Michigan forest fungus weighs at least 22,000 pounds. . . .

Charles Petit, San Francisco *Chronicle*

"You might be on a walk in the woods and see mushrooms a kilometer apart, but most people would never guess they were all part of the same individual."

Myron Smith, graduate student,
University of Toronto, Canada

Miscellaneous Recipes

Mushroom Quiche

Courtesy of Monterey Mushrooms, Santa Cruz, California

To this vegetarian, brunch specialty, add a fresh fruit or green salad. 324 calories per serving.

Pastry for 9-inch one-crust pie

½ lb. fresh white mushrooms, sliced

⅓ cup green bell pepper, chopped

2 tbsp. diet imitation margarine

4 eggs, beaten

1 cup plain lowfat yogurt

2 tbsp. instant minced onion

¾ tsp. salt

⅛ tsp. rubbed sage

⅛ tsp. nutmeg

⅛ tsp. pepper

¾ cup skim milk

¾ cup (3 oz.) shredded swiss cheese

Line 9-inch pie plate with pastry. Flute edge. Set aside. Sauté mushrooms and green pepper in imitation margarine until tender and liquid evaporates. Set aside to cool slightly. Combine eggs, yogurt, onion, salt, sage, nutmeg, and pepper. Stir in milk, cheese, cooked mushrooms, and vegetables. Pour into pastry shell. Bake at 375 degrees about 40 minutes or until knife inserted 1 inch from edge comes out clean, and top is lightly browned. Let stand 15 minutes before seving. Serves 6.

Mom's Treat (Sandwich)

Margaret Whelly and Jim Gongwer,
The First Light Cafe, San Francisco, California

Today's sandwiches don't have to be boring re-runs. Mushrooms transport them into the realm of the light fantastic.

1 cup mushrooms, thickly sliced

1 tbsp. butter

8 slices of fresh whole wheat bread

4 or 5 slices of meat loaf

1 large tomato, thinly sliced

4 leaves butter lettuce

Mayonnaise

Spicy mustard

In a heavy pan or on a grill, sauté mushrooms in butter on high heat until crisp-tender. In a microwave or oven, heat meat loaf slices.

Stack sandwich as follows:

1 slice bread

1 slice meat loaf

2 tomato slices

Sautéed mushrooms

Butter lettuce leaf

Top with 1 slice wheat bread
Serve with mayonnaise or spicy mustard.
Serves 4.

Let Us Indulge (Sandwich)

Margaret Whelly and Jim Gongwer,
The First Light Cafe, San Francisco, California

8 strips of lean, thin bacon, fried
  crisp and drained

4 sandwich slices of jack, muenster
  or mozzarella cheese

1 cup mushrooms, thickly sliced and
  sautéed or grilled

1 large tomato, thinly sliced

4 leaves of butter lettuce

8 slices of fresh wheat bread

Mayonnaise, to taste

Spicy mustard

Stack sandwich as follows:
Place 2 bacon strips on each of 4 slices of
bread. Place cheese slices on top of the
bacon.

Put bacon and cheese-covered bread on a
cookie sheet about 4 inches from flame in
the broiler and broil for 6 or 7 minutes, or
until cheese melts. Remove from broiler
and place separately on 4 plates.

Add mushrooms, 2 tomato slices, and a leaf
of butter lettuce. Serve with mayonnaise
and spicy mustard. Serves 4.

California Obsession (Sandwich)

Margaret Whelly and Jim Gongwer,
The First Light Cafe, San Francisco, California

1 tsp. butter

12 thin slices of zucchini squash,
  each about 4 or 5 inches long

1 cup white mushrooms, thickly
  sliced and dry sautéed until
  crisp-tender

1 large tomato, sliced thinly

4 whole leaves of butter lettuce

8 slices of wheat bread

In a small skillet or on a grill, melt butter
and sauté zucchini on medium heat, both
sides, for about 5 minutes or until
crisp-tender. Set aside to cool slightly.

Build sandwich as follows:
Place 3 zucchini slices on a slice of bread

Cover with ¼ of the mushrooms, 2 slices of
tomato, and 1 leaf lettuce

Add second slice of bread. Serves 4.

Ravishing Rainbow (Sandwich)

Margaret Whelly and Jim Gongwer,
The First Light Cafe, San Francisco, California

Beef Salad
4 thin slices of left-over, cooked beef, chopped

¼ cup red bell pepper, chopped

¼ cup yellow bell pepper, chopped

2 tsp. spicy mustard

1 tbsp. mayonnaise

2 tbsp. red wine vinegar

2 tbsp. onion, finely chopped

Beef Salad Sandwiches
1 fresh large tomato, thinly sliced

1 cup fresh medium white mushrooms, thickly sliced; dry sautéed until crisp-tender

Mayonnaise, to taste

Spicy mustard, to taste

4 whole butter lettuce leaves

8 slices whole wheat bread

In a bowl, combine beef, bell pepper, mustard, mayonnaise, vinegar, and onion.

Build sandwich as follows:
Spread ¼ of Beef Salad on slice of bread.

Cover with ¼ the mushrooms
Add 2 tomato slices and lettuce.
Cover with remaining bread slice. Serves 4.

Pacific Pacifier (Sandwich)

Margaret Whelly and Jim Gongwer,
The First Light Cafe, San Francisco, California

1 tbsp. butter or olive oil

4 (4 oz.) thin fish fillets

8 slices of whole wheat bread

½ lemon

1 cup fresh white mushrooms, thickly sliced and dry sautéed until crisp-tender

1 large tomato, thinly sliced

4 leaves of butter lettuce

Mayonnaise

Spicy mustard

Tartar sauce

In a non-stick, large skillet or on a grill, heat butter or olive oil. Sauté fish fillets over medium-high heat for 5 or 6 minutes, turning once. Remove from heat and drain on a paper towel.

Stack sandwich as follows:
On 1 slice of bread, place 1 fish fillet

Squeeze about ¼ tsp. lemon juice on fillet

Add ¼ mushroom slices, 2 slices of tomato, and 1 lettuce leaf

Add mayonnaise, spicy mustard, and tartar sauce. Add remaining slice of bread. Serve immediately. Serves 4.

Academic Rush (Sandwich)

The First Light Cafe, San Francisco, California

4 extra large eggs

2 tbsp. butter

8 slices wheat bread

4 large slices of cheddar cheese

1 cup fresh white or brown mushrooms, thickly sliced and dry sautéed until crisp-tender

1 large tomato, sliced thinly into 8 slices

4 large leaves of butter lettuce

spicy mustard, to taste

Mayonnaise, to taste

Salt, to taste

Pepper, to taste

In a large, non-stick skillet or on a grill, fry eggs in butter, turning once, until eggs are cooked to medium-well doneness. Set aside on a warm plate covered with a paper towel. Lightly toast bread.

Stack sandwich as follows:
On each bread slice, place 1 fried egg. Cover each egg with a slice of cheese. Place on cookie sheet under the broiler, about 5 inches from flame, for about 5 or 6 minutes, or until cheese melts. Remove from broiler and place egg-cheese bread slices on 4 plates.

To each, add ¼ the mushrooms, 2 tomato slices, and 1 lettuce leaf.

Add spicy mustard, mayonnaise, salt, and pepper, to taste. Serves 4.

Mushroom Macaroon Cookies
Courtesy of Naomi Guthmiller

Mushrooms add a chewy, nutty goodness to these gourmet treats.

½ cup butter or margarine

1 cup brown sugar

1 egg

1 tsp. vanilla

½ tsp. almond extract

2 (1 oz.) squares, unsweetened
  chocolate, melted

2 cups flour

½ tsp. soda

¼ tsp. salt

¾ cup dairy sour cream

½ cup fine macaroon crumbs (from
  4 cookies)

1 cup fresh mushrooms, coarsely
  chopped

Cream butter and sugar until fluffy. Add egg, vanilla, almond extract; beat thoroughly. Stir in chocolate. Sift together flour, soda, salt, and add to creamed mixture alternately with the sour cream. Mix well and add macaroon crumbs and mushrooms. Drop from teaspoon at least 2 inches apart on greased cookie sheet. Bake at 350 degrees for 12 minutes or until done. Makes 4½ dozen cookies.

Mushroom Relish

Courtesy of Monterey Mushrooms, Santa Cruz, California

A delicious accompaniment for barbecued meat. Leftovers keep well in marinade but will darken. 121 calories total.

½ cup water

3 tbsp. apple cider vinegar

1½ tsp. sugar

1 tsp. salt

1 tsp. prepared horseradish

½ bay leaf

½ clove garlic, minced

½ lb. fresh small white mushrooms, sliced

½ cup thinly-sliced red onion rings, separated

Lettuce leaves

Snipped parsley

In small saucepan, combine water, vinegar, sugar, salt, horseradish, bay leaf, and garlic. Simmer, uncovered, 5 minutes. Stir occasionally. Place mushrooms and onions in shallow glass dish. Add liquid. Cover tightly. Refrigerate 2 hours. Stir 2-3 times. Drain and serve in lettuce-lined bowl. Garnish with snipped parsley. Makes about 2 cups.

Mushroom Omelette

Mary Rech, Morgan Hill's Mushroom Mardi Gras Cookoff

A saucy version of an everyday brunch.

Eggs
6 eggs, separated
½ tsp. salt
½ cup sour cream
1 tbsp. margarine

Sauce
½ lb. mushrooms, finely chopped
1 tbsp. margarine
1 tbsp. flour
1 cup chicken broth
¼ cup white wine
Parsley

Eggs
Beat egg whites until stiff. Set aside. Beat egg yolks, until thick and lemon colored. Add salt and sour cream; gently fold into egg whites. Heat 9" skillet. Add 1 tablespoon margarine. Add egg mixture. With edge of teaspoon circle edge of pan, lifting omelette. Brown bottom of omelette about 5 minutes. Fold one half over onto the other half. Cook 2 minutes longer. Serve with sauce.

Sauce
Sauté mushrooms in margarine. Add flour, stirring to blend. Slowly add chicken broth and wine. Stir until sauce thickens. Serve over mushroom omelette. Garnish with parsley.

Notes

Notes

Index

Home Cooking with Mushrooms

Outstanding Recipes from Morgan Hill's Mushroom Mardi Gras, Mushroom Farmers, Families, and Chefs

Buy 5 or more copies and take an additional 20% off the purchase price!
Bonus: $1 off shipping cost for each additional book

Just $14.95

twin falls press

ORDER FORM

☐ **Check**   ☐ **Money Order**

YES! Please Rush Me _____ copies of the book *Home Cooking with Mushrooms* for just **$14.95** each.

Add $3.00 for shipping and tax. Add $2.00 for each additional book ordered.

Name _____

Address _____

_____

City & State _____ Zip _____

Mail Check or Money Order Payable to:
Twin Falls Press
P.O. Box 2001
Morgan Hill, CA 95038